KEY CHALLENGES IN CRIMINAL INVESTIGATION

Martin O'Neill

D1613199

First published in Great Britain in 2018 by

Policy Press
University of Bristol
1-9 Old Park Hill
Bristol
BS2 8BB
UK
t: +44 (0)117 954 5940
pp-info@bristol.ac.uk
www.policypress.co.uk

North America office:
Policy Press
c/o The University of Chicago Press
1427 East 60th Street
Chicago, IL 60637, USA
t: +1 773 702 7700
f: +1 773-702-9756
sales@press.uchicago.edu
www.press.uchicago.edu

British Library Cataloguing in Publication Data
A catalogue record for this book is available from the British Library

Library of Congress Cataloging-in-Publication Data
A catalog record for this book has been requested

ISBN 978-1-4473-2577-2 paperback
ISBN 978-1-4473-2576-5 hardcover
ISBN 978-1-4473-2579-6 ePub
ISBN 978-1-4473-2580-2 Mobi
ISBN 978-1-4473-2578-9 ePdf

The right of Martin O'Neill to be identified as author of this work has been asserted by him
in accordance with the Copyright, Designs and Patents Act 1988.

Cover design by Policy Press
Front cover image kindly provided by Mandy O'Neill/Policy Press
Printed and bound in Great Britain by CMP, Poole
Policy Press uses environmentally responsible print partners

KEY THEMES IN POLICING

Series summary: This textbook series is designed to fill a growing need for titles which reflect the importance of incorporating 'evidence based policing' within Higher Education curriculums. It will reflect upon the changing landscape of contemporary policing as it becomes more politicised, professionalised and scrutinised, and draw out both change and continuities in its themes.

Series Editors: Dr Megan O'Neill, University of Dundee, Dr Marisa Silvestri, University of Kent and Dr Stephen Tong, Canterbury Christ Church University.

Published

Understanding police intelligence work – Adrian James

Plural policing – Colin Rogers

Forthcoming

Miscarriages of justice: Causes, consequences and remedies – Sam Poyser, Angus Nurse and Becky Milne

Practical psychology for policing – Jason Roach

Towards ethical policing – Dominic Wood

Policing the police – Michael Rowe

Police culture – Tom Cockroft

Editorial advisory board

- Paul Quinton (College of Policing)
- Professor Nick Fyfe (University of Dundee)
- Professor Jennifer Brown (LSE)
- Charlotte E. Gill (George Mason University)

In memory of Detective Peter Wakerly

The Arrow and the Song

I shot an arrow into the air,
It fell to earth, I knew not where;
For, so swiftly it flew, the sight
Could not follow it in its flight.

I breathed a song into the air,
It fell to earth, I knew not where;
For who has sight so keen and strong,
That it can follow the flight of song?

Long, long afterward, in an oak
I found the arrow, still unbroke;
And the song, from beginning to end,
I found again in the heart of a friend.

By Henry Wadsworth Longfellow

Contents

List of figures

List of tables

Acronyms and abbreviations

ACCESS	mnemonic for Assess, Collect, Collate, Evaluate, Scrutinise, Summarise
ACPO	Association of Chief Police Officers
APP	Authorised Professional Practice
CB	confirmatory bias
CD	core investigative doctrine
CENTREX	The Centre for Policing Excellence
CCTV	closed circuit television
CID	Criminal Investigation Department
CJA	Criminal Justice Act 2003
CKP	Certificate in Knowledge of Policing
CMM	mnemonic for Conflict Management Model
CoP	College of Policing
CPD	continuing professional development
CPIA	Criminal Procedure and Investigations Act, 1996
CPS	Crown Prosecution Service
DA	domestic abuse
DASH	mnemonic for domestic abuse, stalking and harassment risk assessment tool
DHR	Domestic Homicide Review
DIDP	Detective Inspector Development Programme
ECHR	European Court of Human Rights
EW	England and Wales
FLO	Family Liaison Officer
FOI	Freedom of Information
H2H	house to house
HASC	Home Affairs Select Committee
HCSC	House of Commons Select Committee
HMCPSI	Her Majesty's Crown Prosecution Service Inspectorate
HMIC	Her Majesty's Inspectorate of Constabulary
HOCR	Home Office Counting Rules
HRA	Human Rights Act
ICIDP	Initial Crime Investigator Development Programme
IM	idealised decision-making model
IPA	Investigatory Powers Act 2016
IPCC	Independent Police Complaints Commission
IPLDP	Initial Police Learning and Development Programme
ISDP	Investigative Supervisor Development Programme

JAPAN	mnemonic for Justified, Appropriate, Proportionate, Auditable, Necessary
MIM	Murder Investigation Manual
MIRSAP	Major Incident Room Standard Administrative Procedures
MOJ	miscarriage of justice
MPS	Metropolitan Police Service
MSCIDP	Management of Serious Crime Investigation Development Programme
NCA	National Crime Agency
NCALT	National Centre for Applied Learning Technologies
NCPE	National Centre for Policing Excellence
NDM	National Decision Model
NIE	National Investigators Examination
NOS	National Occupational Standards
NPIA	National Police Improvement Agency
NPCC	National Police Chiefs Council
OET	Outside Enquiry Team
OIOC	Officer in Overall Command
PACE	Police and Criminal Evidence Act 1984
PAQ	Position Analysis Questionnaire
PCA	Police Complaints Authority
PEACE	mnemonic for interview model: Planning and Preparation, Engage and Explain, Account, Closure, Evaluation
PIP	Professionalising the Investigative Process
PLAN	mnemonic for Proportionate, Legitimate, Accountable, Necessary
PLANE	mnemonic for Proportionate, Legitimate, Accountable, Necessary, Ethical
PNLD	Police National Legal Database
PONI	Police Ombudsman of Northern Ireland
POP	Problem Oriented Policing
RAND	research and development organisation from the USA
RASSO	Rape and Serious Sexual Offences (unit)
RIPA	Regulation of Investigatory Powers Act 2000
RCCJ	Royal Commission on Criminal Justice
RCCP	Royal Commission on Criminal Procedure
SARA	mnemonic for Scanning, Analysis, Response, Evaluation
SASI	Self Assessment of Specialist Interviews

SCAIDP   Specialist Child Abuse Investigator Development
            Programme
SIO   Senior Investigating Officer
SIODP   Senior Investigating Officer Development Programme
SOA   Sexual Offences Act 2003
SOIT   Sexual Offence Investigation-Trained
STO   Specially Trained Officer
STODP   Specially Trained Officer Development Programme
THRIVE   mnemonic for Threat, Harm, Risk, Investigation,
            Vulnerability, Engagement
TIC   taken into consideration

Dedication

This book is dedicated to Peter Wakerly, a Kent Police Detective who at work embodied professionalism, and at play had a passion for life and a glint in his eye.

Acknowledgements

Thanks go to Mandy for her endless patience and selflessness, and to Mark and Michael for enriching our lives. Thanks also go to my friends, colleagues and former colleagues for their patience during the writing of this book. Particular thanks go to Dr Paul Gilbert, for endless reflections on research, constant banter and fun. Thanks also to Linda Weeks (Library Lil), as well as usual suspects, Alan and Catherine Thompson, Mario and Donna Theophanous, Adrian and Laurina Moody, David and Susan Greenhill, Karen and John Clark, Chris Collins, Bob Wood, and Antoine Hubert, wherever you are. I bear responsibility for all mistakes contained within this volume.

Series preface

Megan O'Neill, Marisa Silvestri and Stephen Tong

The *Key Themes in Policing* Series aims to support the growing number of policing modules on both undergraduate and postgraduate awards, as well as contribute to the development of policing professionals, including those who wish to join, are new in service or are experienced practitioners. It also seeks to respond to the call for evidence-based policing led by organisations such as the College of Policing in England. By producing a range of high quality, research-informed texts on important areas of policing, contributions to the series support and inform both professional and academic policing curriculums.

Representing the third publication in the series, *Key challenges in criminal investigation* by Martin O'Neill, this book meets all of the series aims. At the time of writing, set against a backdrop of more victims coming forward from historical sexual abuse, increases in terrorist attacks, the challenges of austerity, significant rises in crimes reported to the police, a shortage of detectives and concerns around the wellbeing of detectives – the role of detectives has never been more challenging. This book provides a useful and informative insight into the investigative process and the work of detectives.

Martin O'Neill is a former detective/police trainer and is now a Senior Lecturer in Criminal Investigation at Canterbury Christ Church University. Martin has experience of operational policing, conducting research on detectives and teaching the key components of investigation in university and police training settings. He is very well positioned to deliver a publication of this nature to appeal to experienced police officers as well as students coming across the subject matter for the first time. The publication of this book is timely to build on the limited literature currently available but also to provide a useful text that will support the professionalisation agenda in policing as it evolves. The quality and complexity of criminal investigation continues to be a crucial area for discussion in policing and this book provide a useful and authoritative account of the challenges detectives face. From an outline of what criminal investigation entails, debates around the art, craft and science of investigation, the role of the law and the IPCC, this book selects key themes that will be invaluable to policing scholars. This book will serve as a useful introduction for 'newcomers' studying detective work through to those already in the field, offering a comprehensive analysis of the key challenges in criminal investigation.

Preface

The process of criminal investigation is often described as akin to compiling a jigsaw puzzle. The analogy suggests a crime is meticulously pieced together, to create a picture of what happened. In an ideal world, the picture would include the perpetrator of the crime and, through legal process, some form of justice would follow. However, the analogy does not represent reality. For a start, investigators do not have a picture from which to work. Neither do they have edge pieces that help to define the limits of their inquiry. With a jigsaw puzzle, one can start by finding all the edges, creating the borders and working inwards. The rest of the puzzle can then be slowly pieced together to form the likeness on the box. Real criminal investigations have no such confines. Indeed, it is more fitting to suggest that criminal investigation is like trying to complete a jigsaw puzzle without a picture, without all the pieces and without any parameters. When a jigsaw puzzle is completed, all the pieces are present and all relate to that picture. We *know* the answer is there. In a criminal investigation, not all pieces of evidence are discovered. Witnesses may never come forward; some may lie; victims' accounts might vary in quality (understandably); evidence may be overlooked or ignored; and investigative efforts may vary significantly. Where an investigation uncovers a suspect, there is always a risk that the picture of the crime is only a partial reflection of reality. Nevertheless, it is the picture produced by the investigation, and it is then represented as the prosecution version of the facts. That there can sometimes be injustice is not surprising, even if we accept this simplistic view of the process of investigation. Add to that prosecution wrongdoing, corruption, and victims and witnesses with nefarious motives, and it is not difficult to see why criminal investigation is often fraught with difficulties. This book relates to criminal investigation undertaken by all police investigators, not just detectives. The majority of investigations are low-level volume crimes, undertaken by uniformed or civilian investigators. Serious and complex crimes are dealt with by trained detectives, and, if designated major crimes, they are dealt with by specialist detectives, trained specifically to undertake that role.

This book is informed by existing research and the authors' own research on volume crime investigation undertaken as part of a doctorate with the University of Portsmouth between 2008 and 2011. Policing is now firmly within a paradigm of evidence-based policing practice, the basic tenet of which is that practice should, like other professions, be informed by credible research. As a result, each chapter will consider research strategies and methodologies of selected research. It will become apparent throughout that some areas have received scant attention in contemporary research. Moreover, where research has been completed, it is often descriptive, without suggesting how practice can learn from it. In this book I hope to highlight some gaps in knowledge of criminal investigation, suggesting further research in the exciting times that lie ahead.

Martin O'Neill
Canterbury Christ Church University
2017

ONE

Introduction: Defining criminal investigation

You only have to look at the daily press to read real–life stories involving criminal investigations. The cases reported do not necessarily indicate a rise or fall in crime or in particular crimes, because often the cases reported are noteworthy ones, judged to be of particular public interest by journalists, editors and publishers (Brodeur, 2010). Murders and other violent crimes continue to receive publicity irrespective of whether their rates are rising or falling. It is sometimes difficult to discern what the underlying motives are on the part of the media for publishing particular stories (Reiner, 2008). What publicity does though, is bring criminal investigation to the attention of the public. Add to that the wealth of literature dedicated to crime fiction, and the public's fascination with it, and it is easy to see why criminal investigation is often at the forefront of public consciousness. People appear to love the whodunits, the cases of note, and the way the police sleuth tracks down their prey with skill, intelligence and tenacity. Maybe that idealised picture of an investigation has happened in real, modern-day cases, but much of what is depicted has been shown to be far removed from reality by academic research. Successive studies in the USA in the late 1960s and early 1970s (see, for instance: Isaacs, 1967; Greenwood, 1970; Greenberg et al, 1972) culminated in the much debated RAND study (Greenwood et al, 1977). Combined, these studies challenged myths by concluding that crimes were mostly solved by patrol officers and members of the public, not by detectives. These findings were supported by UK research (Bottomley and Coleman, 1981; Burrows and Tarling, 1987). Indeed, much modern-day investigative practice in the UK involves uniformed officers investigating the highest proportion of crimes (volume crime), leaving detectives to investigate serious and complex, major and serious crimes (Audit Commission, 1993; Burrows et al, 2005). Volume crime management practices are such that they ensure that only cases with good leads are investigated, with a large proportion filed at the time of report (James and Mills, 2012). Far from being an exciting occupation, investigative work is often mundane (Matza, 1969), bureaucratic (Brodeur, 2010), fruitless (Greenwood et al, 1977;

Steer, 1980; Bottomley and Coleman, 1981; Burrows and Tarling, 1987), and better described as an exercise in clearing crimes rather than detecting them (Laurie, 1970). This chapter provides an overview of criminal investigation from three perspectives: the theoretical, the definitional and the doctrinal. First, two theoretical frameworks for thinking about criminal investigations will be considered, providing different lenses through which the process can be viewed. Second, a number of definitions will be discussed, culminating in consideration of the legal context within which criminal investigations are undertaken in the UK. Finally, police doctrine, understood as attempts by the police to define investigative practice, will be outlined. The conclusion to this chapter will also outline the content of other chapters to follow.

Theories of criminal investigation

Innes (2003) and Brodeur (2010) have attempted to articulate theoretical frameworks through which to see the work of detectives. It is to their two constructs that this chapter will turn first, although these themes should be considered as distinct from specific definitions and descriptions of criminal investigation. The two theories help us conceptualise criminal investigations before looking further at definitional issues.

Adopting a predominantly qualitative approach and a sociological perspective, Innes (2003) observed detectives in one police force in the UK, conducting homicide investigations in their working habitus. This research distinguishes Innes's work from studies such as Hobbs (1988), where observations were undertaken predominantly outside the formal work setting (Hallenberg et al, 2015). For a total of five months, Innes observed five murder investigations as they progressed from start to finish over a two-year period. Observations were supplemented by a review of case files (20) and case summaries of completed murder investigations (50). Detectives involved in the 20 cases were also interviewed, and findings were supplemented with a review of existing policies and procedures. Innes was also able to observe detectives working with the Holmes database for a period of three months. This database assists major crime investigations in the management, processing and recording of large amounts of information emanating from a large enquiry. The system was developed following the Byford report (1981) into the Yorkshire Ripper Investigation, which found, among other things, that the police management of large amounts of information in major homicide investigations was woefully inadequate. Innes's mixed methods approach in using all these different research tools also allowed for triangulation of findings at the point of analysis and discussion (Innes, 2003, p 283).

Innes (2003) theorised that criminal investigation was essentially information work (Sanders, 1977; Ericson, 1981; Ericson and Haggerty, 1997), observing that murder squad investigators (as information workers) constructed meaning from events by drawing inferences, and interpreting material. The detective's construction became the official version of what happened, although on any view such a version is likely to reflect the scope and depth of an inquiry, and the amount of information recovered and considered relevant. According to Innes: 'The investigation of crime is fundamentally a form of information work, it is concerned with the identification, interpretation and ordering of information with the objective of ascertaining whether a crime has occurred and if so who was involved and how' (Innes, 2003, p 113).

Innes found that detectives utilised different types of technology while employing investigative methodologies. Investigative methodology informed the two technological processes of producing information and producing knowledge. Innes suggested that technology for producing information included human resources engaged in an investigation (in a major crime, investigators are referred to as the Outside Enquiry Team (OET), interviews, media, House to House enquiries (H2H) enquiries, and intelligence work. Technology for producing knowledge, included forensic work, temporal ordering, and case narratives. Innes posited that the investigative task in homicide investigation primarily involved the search for information. He described a hierarchy of information in relation to investigations. This is demonstrated in Figure 1.1. According to Innes, investigators search for information and distinguish it from 'noise'; that is, irrelevant information (see also Ericson and Haggerty, 1997; James, 2016). Once this task has been undertaken, the remaining information or intelligence is moulded into knowledge and evidence in the process of formulating a case against a suspect. Brodeur and Dupont (2006) suggest that information needs to be validated prior to being acted on. In the world of detectives, the process of marshalling all that is known into the legal niceties of evidence and a plausible case against a suspect is what Innes (2003) terms the social construction of meaning (Berger and Luckmann, 1966). Different meaning is assigned to different types of information, and each piece of information assumes a hierarchy of importance to support (or not) a case theory. Such information work involves making judgements about the nature and quality of the material, and assessing it in conjunction with other information, intelligence, knowledge or evidence already known. Innes (2003) further described how one piece of information could change in importance as an investigation progressed, either becoming more important than first thought, or less important as further information is uncovered. Innes identified the ebb and flow of investigative work, where the more that is uncovered, the more hypotheses are (or should be) generated, and the more work is required to understand the nature of the material at hand and how it relates to other material. Homicide detectives utilise organised structures and practices (including the Holmes system) to assist them in managing the incoming information. They also employ strategies and actions to gain information. The hierarchy in Figure 1.1 is not dissimilar to the ladder of information highlighted by Dean and Gottschalk (2007), with the exception that 'noise' is there described as data, and evidence is understood as the wisdom sought to be achieved within an investigation. On a practical level in England and Wales (EW), the Criminal Procedure and Investigations Act, 1996 (CPIA) regulates how the police should deal with material emanating from a criminal investigation, with investigators deciding between relevance, unused material and evidence. In this sense, 'noise' equates to irrelevant material, while relevant information and intelligence would need to be considered as either evidence or unused material.

Figure 1.1: Hierarchy of information

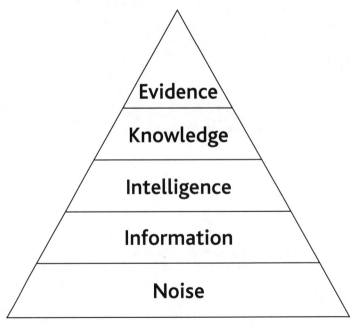

Brodeur (2010) points out that Innes's explanation of knowledge work does not account for all of the nuances of investigation, particularly where offenders are captured 'red-handed' by a rapid police response, or where the public help to solve crimes quickly. Brodeur (2010) suggests that little or no information work is undertaken in these examples, although it may still be necessary post-arrest in order to marshal a case to an appropriate conclusion (i.e. charge, caution, reprimand, etc.). Brodeur (2010) posits that criminal investigation should be viewed in a more pragmatic fashion. He suggests that Innes's theory (and previous research) is wont to ignore the systems and processes that are undertaken post-charge and at court. His own empirical research suggested that much investigative time is spent in attempting to secure convictions. Indeed, other UK commentators have stressed the importance of post-arrest investigative work (see, for instance, Stelfox, 2009). Even where there is a suspect arrested on what appears to be strong evidence, a case still requires significant investigative effort to ensure that it is presented in an evidential format (Chatterton, 2008). In that sense, at some point in the investigative process, the case needs to be constructed for the prosecutor (Innes, 2003). Sanders (1977) conducted participant observation on detectives in the USA for over a year. He also argued that investigators undertook a form of information gathering work, by evaluating information in order to detect crimes. However, his work was predicated on the basis that an arrest acted as a crime clearance. Little was observed in relation to post-arrest case construction. Moreover, the detective work observed was essentially reactive, providing little understanding of the nature of proactive detective work or other forms of investigation (i.e. intelligence work). Bearing in mind that, in jurisdictions such as the UK, USA and Canada, the process of constructing a case for a successful outcome necessarily follows arrest, this is a significant part of investigative practice often neglected by researchers (Tilley et al, 2007; Brodeur, 2010).

Innes (2003) is clear that much investigative work is undertaken at the case construction stage. He argued that all stages of the investigative process, including post-arrest activity, is information work. As an example, he traced the activities of investigations in three homicide cases. The first was an easily solved murder that took four days to complete, the second was a murder that took 11 days, while the third was a more complex case that the police took longer to resolve. Innes tracked the frequency of actions relating to particular aspects of the investigation such as victim activity, suspect activity, and information activity (Innes called this diachronic tracking). In at least two cases, suspects were arrested early in the investigation. Yet Innes demonstrates that information work undertaken by detectives went beyond that stage.

Brodeur's Canadian research gained access to crime cases between 1990 and 2004. The research aimed to discover how crimes were solved and the part that knowledge played. The study set out to compare solved cases with unsolved cases and analysed 25 cases relating to narcotics, sexual offences, robbery, fraud and homicide. Regrettably, there was a dearth of information in most of the crime files, some having only a few lines of material. The only cases that had detailed information within them were the homicide cases, presumably because of the importance attached to those investigations, and the need for a more accountable and auditable process. Analysis of the non-homicide cases led Brodeur to concur with the conclusion of previous studies that crimes were solved for reasons other than investigative effort (Ericson, 1981; Greenwood et al, 1977).

Brodeur and Dupont (2006) recognise that there are some systemic issues with information work. They note the tendency for there to be tensions between the police and national security agencies, who do not have the same focus on court cases and convictions as the sole arbiter of success. They will often be reluctant to provide information to the police that they do not believe to be in their interests to share. There is a belief that the police are overloaded with information, making it difficult for them to distinguish between noise and information (Sheptycki, 2004).

Brodeur (2010) developed a typology of investigations by identifying nine different types of investigations undertaken by the police. Table 1.1 is an elaboration of Brodeur's thoughts, with the addition of integrated investigation (having identified this type of investigation, he felt this had no place within his typology). The different types of investigation can be distinguished (by their method used), into reactive, proactive, retrospective or integrated. Brodeur (2010) added to two classic criminal investigation distinctions, that of proactive and reactive investigations (Kuykendall, 1987). Proactive investigations concern activities (usually covert) designed to capture a suspect in the act of committing the crime, or implicating a criminal in a crime in some fashion, whether by association with other criminals in a conspiracy or any other reason (Tong et al, 2009). This type of example is most likely to relate to the preventive section of Table 1.1, where the focus is proactive and suspect centred. Brodeur's nine types of investigations are highlighted in bold.

Table 1.1: Brodeur typologies (amalgamated)

Method/type	Suspect-centred	Event-centred	Hybrid
Proactive	**Preventive** (e.g. counterterrorism)	**Special high-security events**	**Instigation** (e.g. sting operations)
Reactive	**Individual**	**Current case solving**	**Post-case processing**
Retrospective	**Security clearance**	**Assessment of suspicious events**	**High-profile suspect**
Integrated	High-profile serial investigation – suspect known but not yet located	High-profile serial investigation	

Source: Adapted from Brodeur, 2010

Reactive investigations are those that usually come to mind if the public are asked to describe a typical crime investigation. Here is the familiar investigation instigated by a report to the police from a member of the public, with the police working to find the perpetrator (Tong et al, 2009). Brodeur (2010) adds retrospective investigations to the classic dichotomy. He identifies this kind of investigation as exploring whether past actions or events were criminal. One example is the Libor bank scandal in the UK, in which the actions of bank staff became the subject of criminal investigation when there were suggestions that they were involved in rigging the Libor market. Another example is the investigation into the activities of Jimmy Savile, undertaken after his death to ascertain the nature of his criminal offending. Whether these types of inquiry are distinct enough from a reactive inquiry to merit a separate label is arguable. Both the Libor and Savile cases are examples of information coming to light that demands an investigation. As Brodeur points out, in these cases a suspect is already known and the investigation serves to discover whether there is any criminality attached to their behaviour. Is this not just another form of reactive inquiry? Admittedly, the retrospective inquiry is something that has grown significantly in the UK lately. One only has to look in the news to see investigations fitting this criterion involving famous entertainers (i.e. Savile, Harris), and high-profile public figures (various former Members of Parliament). These cases have sexual offences as the focus of investigation, but one can also add high-profile cases such as Hillsborough to the growing list of examples. Because of the proliferation of these retrospective investigations and the wealth of resources required to undertake them, there are interesting pragmatic questions as to whether they are sustainable within current police budgets, although the clamour for answers in the public interest will often override such objections. Indeed, in the case of Savile, the inquiry was important to uncover any living accomplice who may still have had access to children. Child protection is often a critical concern in historical sexual abuse investigations.

The final facet discussed by Brodeur, although not placed within his typology, was that of integrated investigations. These are high-profile cases such as serial murders. Brodeur suggests that these types of cases were usually investigated by a task force consisting of personnel from different jurisdictions. In the UK, the Yorkshire Ripper investigation would be a good example of this type of investigation (Byford, 1981). Integrated investigation has been added to the above table, as it is posited that these kinds of investigation can also have a similar range of methodological perspectives to other types of investigations. Brodeur's discussion highlights the potential for a different focus depending on the perspective adopted.

Brodeur (2010) suggested that any investigation could have three different perspectives: suspect-centred, event-centred and hybrid. Traditional criminal investigations can be characterised as those that involve the report of a crime, followed by investigation to discover who committed it. In effect, investigation from the crime to the suspect. This would constitute what Brodeur considers to be an event-focused investigation. This can be seen in Table 1.1, labelled 'Current case solving' (circled). Suspect-centred approaches are by definition very different. The starting point is a suspect, and investigation is undertaken to link the suspect to a crime or crimes they may be suspected of, or to discover whether they have committed offences and, if so, how many. The hybrid investigation encompasses a mixture of both event- and suspect-centred investigations. Brodeur makes no grand claims for his typology. He accepts that there are many cases that do not fit the distinctions completely. For instance, cases may begin as event-centred, and later become suspect-centred. This will be true in the UK in the majority of cases, in which a suspect is identified and a case file is required to seek the permission of CPS for a charge or other disposal. In addition, some cases may begin as reactive inquiries, but they may employ proactive means to assist in evidence gathering. Such investigations may fluctuate between suspect-centred and event-centred.

Building on Brodeur's typologies, it is suggested that a further dimension could be added to this understanding. In the UK, crimes are categorised as volume, serious or major crimes, depending on their seriousness. Volume crimes are afforded a different level of investigation to serious and major crime (Harfield, 2008). As will be discussed later in Chapter 3, the Professionalising of the Investigative Process (PIP) aligns to this distinction in terms of case seriousness. Qualified PIP level one investigators deal with volume crime investigations, PIP level two-qualified individuals deal with serious and complex cases, while PIP level three-qualified manage major crime investigations (Stelfox, 2009; Tong et al, 2009). PIP level four-qualified investigators manage investigations that involve major cross-border crimes, such as the Yorkshire Ripper investigation, should such an investigation be undertaken in the modern era. Each level of crime designation brings with it resources commensurate with the perceived seriousness of the crime. In common parlance, this would be considered to be a proportional response to the level of crime being investigated. As a result of this discussion, Figure 1.2 represents different dimensions of criminal investigations. These accommodate Brodeur's considerations with the addition of three levels of crime seriousness. These also cater for the integrated investigations discussed by Brodeur, which would be likely to inhabit the seriousness level of 'major crime'. As Sanders (1977) observed, not only is crime seriousness important for operational and resource considerations, it has often been a signal of the status of detectives among peers. The more important the case, the more credibility is afforded an investigator.

Behind each dimension in Figure 1.2 sit a range of practices, policies and considerations that assist to conceptualise practice. As an example, in modern investigations, the College of Policing (CoP) assert the importance of decision-making, and they encourage the recording of rationale (CoP, 2017a). Decisions as to seriousness, method and perspective are important at the start of an investigation, and such decisions shape the course of the inquiry. Following this, a wealth of further strategic and tactical decisions are made, depending on the stage and complexity of the investigation (Innes, 2003; Stelfox, 2009; Tong et al, 2009; Cook and Tattersall, 2014). Brodeur (2010) observes that some arrests are made at the time a crime is committed, and the investigation moves directly into the suspect management phase. While this is a criminal investigation, it is very different from the classic example of a crime report, followed by investigation, followed by the uncovering of a suspect. Indeed, this discussion demonstrates that theorising about criminal investigation is still very much in its infancy. As Brodeur (2010) suggests, a theory of the criminal investigation *process* may be distinct from a theory of *solving* crimes, and such a theory has yet to be fully articulated.

Figure 1.2: Dimensions of criminal investigation

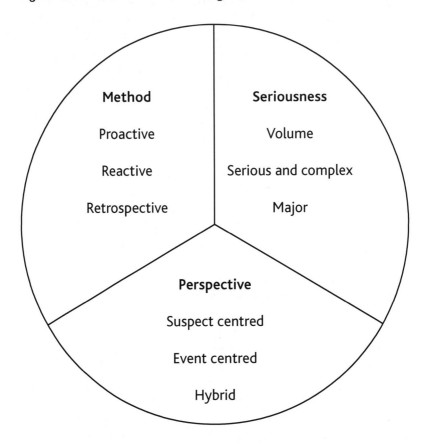

Defining criminal investigation

There are at least three different perspectives involved in previous attempts to define the term 'criminal investigation'. Some attempt to describe it in terms of what it is, others attempt to define it in terms of what it ought to be, while uniquely in the UK there is a normative definition provided by the Criminal Procedure and Investigations Act, 1996 and associated codes of practice. This provides the most important practical definition for investigators in that it defines part of the legal context within which criminal investigations must be undertaken in England and Wales (EW). The next section will discuss just a few of many definitions that exist in relation to the term 'criminal investigation'.

One enduring question within contemporary academic literature has been whether criminal investigation is an art, craft or science, and which one of these is practised by investigators when undertaking their investigations (Repetto, 1978; Innes 2003; Tong and Bowling, 2006; O'Neill, 2011; Westera et al, 2014). This question will be discussed further in Chapter 2. As a starting point, Harfield (2008) defines criminal investigation as: 'the scientific collection, examination and preservation of evidence. Because it is a costly and resource-intensive procedure, a thorough investigation cannot be applied to all reported crimes. Hence, the strategic categories of volume and serious crime are used to determine where and how investigation resources are allocated' (Harfield, 2008, p 67).

There is no clear definition of the term 'scientific' here in the context of criminal investigation. What does the definition mean? Does it claim the process of criminal investigation as science? In what sense is it legitimate to make this claim for criminal investigation? This will be discussed further, particularly in light of suggestions that criminal investigations take place in a more scientific-orientated era. The second and third paragraphs of the definition identify a pragmatic approach to high-volume crime investigations, making it clear that less serious cases will not be investigated as thoroughly as more serious cases. Written in 2008, the definition has even more resonance with the reality of the situation in austerity, when resources are scarce. That said, it raises interesting questions about the nature of modern criminal investigations and public expectations. Many volume crime cases are filed without any investigative effort being expended, by way of a screening process. Those cases deemed low solvability will be recorded and filed. Other cases will receive minimal investigative effort, and they will be investigated by officers trained to investigate volume crimes. In the modern era, these investigations will usually be undertaken by uniformed officers. In theory, more serious cases (serious and complex) will be allocated to qualified detectives. In theory, these will be investigated more thoroughly. One of the most important points that this cursory discussion raises is the fact that criminal investigations include the whole ambit of criminal offences from the least serious to the most serious, and a whole range of levels of investigator can be called on to lead such investigations. The myth that criminal investigation is the sole purview of detectives has been consistently shown to be exactly that (Stelfox, 2009). What is also striking is the fact that the detection of a theft of a bar of chocolate is accorded the same detection score as a murder. Both crimes (if solved) would count as a single detection, when the investigative effort involved in the theft would be minimal compared to the murder, and the murder is clearly more significant in terms of loss of life, public protection and public perception of police competence. Such counting of detections also provides a somewhat false positive in relation to the nature, quality and seriousness of crimes solved, and says little about the level of resources deployed to do so.

Some textbooks tend to concentrate on investigation as an ex post facto inquiry (Osterburg and Ward, 2000; Weston and Lushbaugh, 2012). As an example, Osterburg and Ward (2000) suggest that criminal investigation is 'The reconstruction of past events' (cited by Osterburg and Ward (2000) as a personal communication, p 5). The definition appears to encompass all criminal investigations, providing as it does a simple suggestion that after crime occurs, the criminal investigation attempts to reconstruct what has happened. However, it is clear that there are other perspectives involved in criminal investigation. As will be seen from the UK legal definition below, criminal investigations specifically include investigations begun in the belief that crimes will occur in the future. Some proactive investigations attempt to capture criminals in the act of committing crimes, and such proactive investigations are by definition criminal investigations (CPIA, 1996a). As is clear from the previous discussion of Brodeur (2010), describing criminal investigation based on the dominant assumption that all investigations focus from a crime event to the capturing of a suspect ignores some very important criminal investigation perspectives. Criminal investigation is much more sophisticated and multi-faceted than that, and to that extent this definition fails to reflect this. As Brodeur suggests, some investigations begin at the point of arrest where an offender is caught in the act of committing a crime. The investigative activity is no more than finding evidence in order to build the case against that suspect. This is not merely a form of reconstructing past events, but something much more focused on the suspect because of the specific circumstances of the case. Indeed, Brodeur's typologies come into their own here, allowing us to reflect on the type of case that it is, whether suspect-centred, event-centred or hybrid, as well as what particular methods are employed (proactive, reactive, etc.), and the level of seriousness of the case, which may define the resources available to it. Brown (2001, p 3) provides a definition that encompasses both past and present investigation by asserting: 'Criminal Investigation is the process of legally gathering evidence of a crime that has been or is being committed'. Rossomo (2008) suggests that the criminal investigation process involves two stages. The first revolves around identifying the offender, while the second involves proving the offender's guilt. This ignores one of the fundamental starting points of an investigation that tends to determine whether a person is deemed to be suitable for the services of the criminal justice system, and, if they are, whether that service is likely to be a good or bad one. What Rossomo does, however, is discuss this definition in conjunction with miscarriages of justice. Miscarriages of justices (MOJs) will commonly occur, according to Rossomo, when investigators assume guilt and enter the second stage of the process too early (this will be discussed in more detail in Chapter 4).

Finally, Stelfox (2009) attempts to define UK criminal investigations from a broader perspective, encompassing aims for an investigation not solely conditional on conviction. Indeed, he situates investigation as information work. He suggests: 'Whatever level of offending it is directed at, criminal investigation involves locating, gathering and using information to bring offenders to justice or to achieve one of the other objectives set for it by the police service, such as victim care, intelligence gathering or managing crime' (Stelfox, 2009, p 1) It is clear from this brief summary of definitions of criminal investigation that opinions vary as to how it should and could be defined. However, from a practitioner point of view, any theories and definitions of criminal investigation, while important for a greater understanding of the milieu, pale into insignificance when compared to the legal definition which defines and mandates particular practices and procedures within criminal investigations. The next section discusses the importance of that definition to practitioners.

The statutory definition

Disclosure in the EW criminal justice system has been dogged by problems, controversy and failure. Some would argue that this is not surprising, bearing in mind how the process has often relied on the prosecution to disclose material that might assist an accused in mounting their defence (Auld, 2001; Taylor, 2006). This is anathema to the adversarial process within the UK criminal justice system as well as to the cultural beliefs of police practitioners, some of whom still appear to elevate crime control above due process in their working lives (Taylor, 2006). MOJ cases have demonstrated how 'disclosure' has often been at the heart of failed investigations. The cases of Judith Ward (1993), R v Kiszco (1992), and the Taylor sisters (1994) are just a few examples of how disclosure malpractice led to MOJs, either where wrongful convictions occurred, or where potentially guilty suspects went unpunished (Leng and Taylor, 1996; Niblett, 1997; Savage and Milne, 2007; Poyser and Milne, 2015). The Government's response to these failings, highlighted by the Royal Commission on Criminal Justice (1993), was to put in place the statutory regime for disclosure in the form of the CPIA, 1996 and its associated codes of practice.

Heavily influenced by the police and a crime control agenda, the statutory regime arguably puts even more emphasis on the police and prosecution supplying information to the defence that might assist their case (Sharpe, 1999; Taylor, 2001; Taylor, 2006). However, this time, it is undertaken on a statutory footing, one that outlines the specific legal duties of the police, the prosecutor and the defence.

It is important to stress the practical effect of the new regime on police investigations. The Act catered for disclosure by the prosecutor in certain circumstances, together with obligations for the defence to submit a defence case statement (CPIA, 1996a). The Codes of Practice, on the other hand, were designed to regulate police conduct in relation to material as soon as a criminal investigation began. The Codes of Practice therefore goes further than regulating police conduct vis-à-vis unused prosecution material. They include provisions designed to ensure that police investigations are carried out in an objective manner. One particular provision in the codes requires officers to follow 'all reasonable lines of enquiry whether they point towards or away from the suspect' (Paragraph 3.1, CPIA Code of Practice, 1996b). What the Act does is regulate police activity from the start of a criminal investigation, in order to ensure fairness of action and objectivity in the whole process, not just at the disclosure stage. Whether this has had the desired effect is disputed (Leng and Taylor, 1996; Taylor 2006), and there is a some evidence to suggest that it has not (Taylor, 2006).

All of the duties falling on the police in relation to the Codes of Practice only apply if a criminal investigation has begun. The Act and Codes of Practice together define what a criminal investigation is. The definition states that criminal investigations begin even where police suspect that someone is going to commit a future crime and undertake some proactive work such as surveillance, as well as when investigations are conducted into crimes already committed. Additionally, investigations conducted to find out *whether* a crime has occurred are also within the ambit of the definition. What does this mean? If a police officer is called, for example, to the death of a worker on a building site, is *that* a criminal investigation at the point at which the police are trying to ascertain whether a crime has been committed or not? It appears that it is.

In accord with the earlier discussion (indicating that uniformed police, civilians and detectives all investigate crime at various levels of complexity), the CPIA codes define the term 'investigator' to include anyone engaged in a criminal investigation. This makes it clear that all of these roles and ranks have legal duties once a criminal investigation has begun. Once any criminal investigation is in train, investigators have duties under the Act and codes to record and retain relevant material (and ultimately reveal it to the prosecutor). It is easy to understand why the law was set out in this manner. Historic cases demonstrated that the police would often focus on one suspect and find as much material as they could against that individual. Any material suggesting an alternative to their version (for instance alibi material, contrary forensic results, different accounts from witnesses), would be ignored, and later hidden from the defence (Leng and Taylor, 1996; Niblett, 1997). The law now makes it clear that material should be recorded and retained even if it does not incriminate the current suspect, providing it has some relevance to the case at hand. The term 'material' is interesting because it does not distinguish between data, information and intelligence described in Figure 1.1 above. 'Material' in the legal sense would encompass all these different types of information. These would need to be recorded and retained within a criminal investigation if interpreted as relevant, although the power is in the hands of the police to decide relevance, and this can be criticised bearing in mind the historical context.

Returning to the death investigation on the building site, if the death is considered to engage no criminal liability, for instance because it is deemed an unfortunate accident where no living party is considered culpable, then it is no longer treated as a criminal investigation, and the death would most likely be dealt with as a report to the Coroner. Because it is a death investigation also conducted on behalf of the Coroner, the relevant material collected by the police could be useful for any report. In less serious cases, where a decision has been made that there is no longer potential criminal liability, it is likely that any recording of relevant enquiries and material is at that stage scaled down so that the material captured by the cursory investigation is minimal. This is the pragmatic solution. Only if the crime is established and a decision has been made to investigate will the full task of recording and retaining relevant material be considered necessary.

Police doctrine

Historically, very little was written down regarding best practice in crime investigation (Moore and Rubin, 2014). In the early years of crime detection, the craft appeared to be passed down from generation to generation by a process of socialisation, experience and a modicum of training from experienced colleagues. What existed as guidance for the aspiring detective were memoirs published by successful detectives since retired, often edited to accentuate skills utilised and the exciting nature of the work (Shpayer-Makov, 2011). In 1881, the Metropolitan Police Commissioner Howard Vincent published a guide to criminal investigators, incorporating Metropolitan Police Orders and legislation of the day. Included in the guidance were practical tips for officers taxed with particular incidents (e.g. sudden deaths, murders, vagrancy, drunkenness). Vincent's code was in print for more than 50 years and enjoyed good support (Bell and Wood, 2015). Textbooks on criminal investigation were also minimal, with the famous Hans Gross text, *Criminal investigation: A practical handbook for magistrates, police officers and lawyers*, being generally available from 1906 onwards (Moore and Rubin, 2014). This incorporated more than law and procedure, weaving in practical tips, expert advice, psychological principles for interviewing, and scientific principles relating to scene searches (Gross, 1906). Consequently, the book became the staple for criminal investigators in the UK, although its main drawback was its generic nature, with few references to UK law (Moore and Rubin, 2014). In the 1920s, *Moriarty's police law* (Williams, 1929) emerged as a modern replacement for Vincent's code (Bell and Wood, 2015). However, even a later proliferation of textbooks on criminal investigation appeared to lack the distinctiveness of professional doctrine. That is, a distillation of best practice to assist aspiring investigators and current practitioners to carry out their duties. A recurring flaw in the previous system of 'learning on the job' was the issue of failing to capture knowledge from previous practitioners. This led to the cyclical pattern of a detective learning their trade through experience, making mistakes along the way, improving their practice and then retiring. When a new investigator began, they would repeat the same cycle. They would make the same mistakes as previous investigators because they would be starting from a low knowledge base. Little had been formally captured as best practice in over 150 years of investigative work, increasing the craft mentality of the role, and continuing to allow it to be shrouded in mystery (see Chapter 2 for further discussion).

In the late 1990s, there was a perception among senior police officers that a problem loomed. The senior investigating officers of the time were due to retire. The essence of experience in major crime investigations was about to be lost. In addition, the Macpherson report had highlighted the need for improvement in major crime investigation (Macpherson, 1999). To insure against this, the *Murder Investigation Manual* was commissioned by ACPO and was published in its first incarnation in 1998 (ACPO, 2006). This attempted to distil best practice. In 2001, the Home Office suggested that the investigation of homicide should be held up as the gold standard for the investigation of all crimes (Home Office, 2001b). In 2005, following on from the perceived success of the MIM, the *Core Investigative Doctrine* (CD) was produced (ACPO, Centrex, 2005). This aimed to provide a similar guide for investigators conducting investigations at the level of volume and serious crime, and it incorporated many of the processes and practices from the MIM. Within CD, a process map of a typical investigation was produced, and individual chapters described in detail the particular actions strategies and thought processes that an officer could choose to engage, depending on the nature of the investigation and their position within it. These investigative models will be discussed in more detail in Chapter 4, but it is worthy of note that the CD was subsumed into the CoP Authorised Professional Practice (APP) area of the CoP website in 2012. The APP contains guidance in relation to all policing activities, including all levels of criminal investigation, critical incident management, armed policing, covert investigations, intelligence management and civil emergencies. The public-facing website includes much of the guidance, although some material is sensitive and only available to serving police officers.

Conclusion

This chapter has attempted to contextualise criminal investigation by first of all considering why exploration of this subject is relevant in the modern era. Moreover, it has discussed some tentative theoretical frameworks for criminal investigation. Definitions of the term 'criminal investigation' have also been discussed from differing perspectives: these may be of interest to the criminal investigation scholar, but the definition provided in CPIA sets the current legislative context within which police investigators must work in EW. While primarily concerned with recording, retention, revelation to the prosecutor and disclosure of unused material to the defence, the CPIA codes also provide expectations of the level and objectivity with which such investigations should be undertaken. All of these duties arise when a criminal investigation is engaged. There has also been brief consideration of attempts by the police to define investigative practice in the form of practitioner guidance. A form of doctrine, distilled from police practice and with a measure of what Tong et al (2009, p 37) call 'cultural borrowing' has become more prevalent in the modern era, although its relevance, effectiveness and provenance are open to question.

This introduction provides a useful backdrop to the chapters that follow. Chapter 2 will discuss the historical development of detectives from their earliest incarnation to the modern era, discussing how research has influenced the debate around the detective as artisan, craftsman or professional. Modern debates suggest a move away from the art and craft of detective work to a new science-based professionalism. The chapter discusses criminal investigation development, together with the current position, particularly in the light of government austerity measures.

Chapter 3 consolidates Chapter 2 by discussing the historical development of detectives through training and education. With an increasing emphasis on professionalisation of policing together with a new ethical framework, this chapter discusses development of investigative training with reference to the Professionalising Investigation Programme (PIP) that accompanied CD in the early part of the century. Investigators at all levels are 'taught' to National Standards. Technology, in the form of e-learning, is widely used to train and educate staff, in line with similar developments in the educational world. This chapter asks, is there a real journey towards professionalism or do these changes flatter to deceive?

Chapter 4 explores decision-making within criminal investigations, from volume crime through to major and serious crime investigations. Research on confirmatory bias, tunnel vision and cognitive traps will be briefly explored, and the chapter will go on to discuss models of investigation currently within CD and MIM, as well as their underpinning theories and rationale. The National Decision-Making Model (NDM) ratified by the Association of Chief Police Officers (ACPO) in 2012 will be critically analysed, together with its underpinning rationale. This chapter considers whether the NDM is appropriate for all police decision-making and encourages further research to determine whether this is the case. Decision-making failures will also be discussed.

Much has been written about the detective and the law. Chapter 5 discusses the centrality of law to modern criminal investigative practice. Previous studies have criticised the training of 'black letter' law to the exclusion of skills and discretionary conduct. Detective training has ceded to these views to the point where arguably the law is peripheral to investigative training. Training courses are now streamlined and have little time to consider legal issues. While recognising that discretion, and investigative skills are very important to effective investigative practice, this chapter considers the sense in which legal knowledge has been used in a negative fashion, as well as the more professional focus that knowledge of the law can bring to practice. These discussions raise some important questions, such as: How much *should* an investigator know? How *deep* should that knowledge be? How *do* investigators acquire that knowledge?

Chapter 6 considers investigative success in terms of how it has traditionally been measured and how it is currently measured, not only on a strategic level but also in relation to individual investigators and investigations. The wider debate around success and effectiveness is discussed, together with consideration of future measurement in the age of austerity and increasing accountability, as well as public scrutiny.

Chapter 7 discusses Waddington's (2015) suggestion that the police fail to learn lessons from past failings and use the rhetoric of 'learning lessons' to nullify criticism. Accordingly, little changes in relation to police practice in reality. This chapter examines published IPCC investigations, comparing two six-year time periods. Looking at both individual and organisational recommendations, the chapter discusses emerging themes, and specifically considers areas that appear to recur over time.

The concluding remarks will reflect on the previous chapters and discuss the challenges within the field of criminal investigation such as recruitment and training of investigators, decision-making, risk assessment and evidence-based practice within the context of continuing austerity.

Further reading
Brodeur, J.P. (2010) *The policing web*. Oxford: Oxford University Press.
Innes, M. (2003) *Investigating murder: Detective work and the police response to criminal homicide*. Oxford: Oxford University Press.
Taylor, C.W. (2006) *Criminal investigation and pre-trial disclosure in the United Kingdom. How detectives put together a case*. Lampeter: Edwin Mellen Press Ltd.

TWO

Art, craft, science and austerity

Introduction

No discussion of the development of criminal investigation can be divorced from its early roots. We have already seen that historically, criminal investigation was viewed as the sole province of detectives, although rising crime soon led to greater uniformed involvement. Today, the majority of volume crimes are dealt with by uniformed officers, with detectives dealing with serious, complex, and major crimes. This chapter discusses a move away from perceptions of the detective as artist or craftsman towards a more modern professional scientific paradigm. What is known as the 'art, craft, science' debate around detective work receives attention, particularly as the direction of change seems to point to a new era of professionalism unencumbered by the myths and stereotypes that dogged detective work until academic research paved the way for its reassessment. Any perceived march towards professionalisation, however, needs to be considered in light of ongoing government austerity measures since 2011. In 2012, CoP became the professional body for policing, designed to marshal in a new era of professionalisation. Together with a code of ethics, a new accent on approved professional practice, and a paradigm shift to evidence-based policing practice, the developments appear to herald real change. Recent research provides a snapshot of the effects of austerity on police investigations. This chapter traces the development of investigative work and asks whether the rhetoric of professionalisation can survive in austerity.

There has been some debate in the past about whether criminal investigation can be characterised as an art, a craft, or a science (Repetto, 1978; Tong and Bowling, 2006). Much of the debate stems from the fact that detectives were traditionally viewed as artists or craftsmen who learnt their trade by experience and who had innate qualities making them effective. Such considerations raised the old nature–nurture debate about whether good investigators are born or whether the role can be taught, in what is traditionally considered to be a form of work led by innate qualities. In that sense, one could argue that the art, craft, science dimensions can be used to help us understand

21

the historical progression of detective work from its early incarnation (art and craft) to the more modern perspective of professionalisation (science). To what extent the development demonstrates a move to a more scientific approach will also be discussed in light of the distinction between experience-based perceptions of professionalism and the standard perception of it (Gundhus, 2012). The three dimensions can also help us conceptualise what parts of investigative practice require investigators to utilise any of these dimensions in their work. For instance, when a detective is questioning a witness, do they engage their scientific/professional knowledge of how to ask the correct questions? Do they employ some art or craft-like qualities to extract information? What is the nature of the proportion of the work that can be described as artful, craft-like or scientific?

Historical perspective

Repetto (1978), considered art, craft, and science when discussing issues arising from one of the most hotly debated pieces of research conducted into detective practices. Called the RAND study, the research was undertaken in the USA in the mid-1970s in order to ascertain what the process of investigative work entailed, including what led to crimes being cleared (Greenwood et al, 1977). The research methodology has often been criticised, as have the representativeness and generalisability of the findings. Most notably, criticism suggested that the authors of the report had little knowledge of investigative work and that this was evident in their findings and recommendations. The two-year study, supported by the Department of Justice, had four key aims, all designed to understand the investigative process in the USA. The research aimed to describe current practice and organisation of investigations throughout the country, assess the effectiveness of investigations in detection of crimes, and assess the effectiveness of new technologies within criminal investigation, all with a view to judging whether these criteria were affected by department size, geographical location or organisation (Greenwood et al, 1977).

The research began with an organisational questionnaire sent to police departments throughout the USA. Because of the size of the research team and budgetary constraints, a decision was made to concentrate on police departments employing more than 150 officers and covering a population size of more than 100,000. As a consequence, 300 police departments were identified, 231 of which were classed as City Police departments. Questionnaires were sent by post to the police chief of each department with a covering letter asking for responses.

The questions covered the whole of the investigative process from crime scene to clearance, investigation training, case assignments, department size, organisation and characteristics, and evaluation of investigative performance. The study reported 153 returns from police departments (51% response rate). From the 153 responses, a number of police departments were selected for further research. In these areas, the police chief or deputy was interviewed, and observation, interviews and informal discussions took place with investigators over a number of days while they undertook investigations or during training. In addition to amassing a large amount of field notes and interview data, the study obtained statistical data from a number of the police departments, and data on 296 of the 300 police departments from the FBI (data such as size of department, and statistics on cases such as homicide in the year 1972).

Greenwood et al (1977), discovered widespread disparity in operational practices in investigation, clearance, and investigator selection and training. Overall, 78% of investigators were employed in a reactive role, with the remainder involved in specialist investigations such as vice, narcotics, organised crime and surveillance. Over half (58%) of departments had organisational practices where uniformed police officers acted as a first-response capacity to crimes and then handed them on to investigators. The study suggested that detective effort could affect outcomes post-charge (i.e. in what the UK would now call the case management phase), particularly if they had links to prosecutor departments and if they were more thorough in their approach to post-case clearance. They compared two jurisdictions in order to see if there was a link between thoroughness and conviction rates. They derived a set of evidential questions that would ensure that a case was more likely to be successful. They then compared how thorough the two jurisdictions were in relation to the questions. In the more thorough jurisdiction, 45% of the evidential items were present, whereas in the less thorough jurisdiction, 26% were present. The more thorough jurisdiction had a much higher conviction rate. As well as thoroughness, the authors observed that proactive units were more effective in combating crimes such as burglary and robbery, providing staff were well resourced and supported. Repetto (1978) clarified that RAND had not suggested that all detective effort had little effect on crime detections; they had identified some areas of good practice, such as specialist squads.

Overall, however, Greenwood et al (1977), concluded that little detective effort actually solved crimes. What solved crimes was either the efforts of patrol officers, or evidence from victims and witnesses.

Developing that point further, the authors suggested that investigative effort made a difference to detections in only 10% of cases. This led the authors to suggest that many detectives could be moved to different roles with little appreciable difference to crime detection rates. As patrol officers conducted preliminary investigation in the majority of cases, their role could be extended so that cases could be filed earlier with no need to involve specialist investigators. It was also suggested that many of the routine tasks of investigative work could be undertaken by clerical workers rather than detectives. Greenwood et al (1977) also criticised prominent criminal investigation textbooks (e.g. O'Hara, 1970) for continuing to promulgate the idea of detective work as an art. The authors preferred to situate investigative work in a more scientific dimension. Williams and Sumrall (1982, p 122) later observed: 'The detective mystique as a crime solver must be destroyed – they are case managers.' Despite the furore caused by the publication of the RAND study, research since then has tended to support the finding that detective effort does little to detect crime (for the UK, see studies such as: Crust, 1975; Zander, 1979; Steer, 1980; Bottomley and Coleman, 1981; Burrows and Tarling, 1987; for Canada, see: Ericson, 1993; Brodeur, 2010; and for the USA, see: Bloch and Weidman, 1976; Greenberg et al, 1972; Williams and Sumrall, 1982). Burrows and Tarling (1987), for instance, suggest that the police merely process rather than detect crime. However, the idea of a detection or case clearance is different in both the USA and the UK. In the USA at the time of the RAND research, case clearance was the arrest of a person for a crime (Manning, 1977). In fact, the authors even found disparity here, with some police departments claiming case clearances on the basis of recovery of a stolen vehicle, even without an arrest (Greenwood et al, 1977). In the UK, a case is classified as detected when several possible outcomes of an investigation apply. As Tilley et al (2007), suggest, the research focus on investigations has tended to be from the point of a report of crime to an outcome designated by the particular criminal justice system. Little account has been taken of the work instrumental in taking cases to court following charge. Commentators suggest that this is not only a critical and skilful part of detective practice (Stelfox, 2009) but that it is similarly an under-researched area (Brodeur, 2010). Brodeur concurs with Williams and Sumrall, suggesting that detectives are more akin to case managers than detectives seen in a classic sense. Responses to the RAND study were scathing, particularly from senior officers within the police service (Greenwood, 1979; Williams and Sumrall, 1982) although Greenwood noted that officers without criminal investigation experience appeared to accept the findings more readily because they accorded with their own views of what detective work really involved (Greenwood, 1979).

Repetto (1978) sought to establish whether police departments had taken cognisance of the RAND findings by redeploying investigative resources where it might be most effective. RAND had suggested that a large number of investigators could be redeployed with little effect on crime clearances. Repetto expected to find a decline in numbers, but was surprised to find the opposite. In fact, 13% of police departments reported a decline in detective numbers, while 31% had increased. In over half of the departments (56%), detective numbers remained static. While it could be interpreted that the majority of police departments appeared to ignore the prevailing research, over 58% had reported forming task forces (i.e. burglary, robbery and homicide squads). Repetto described an experiment in Rochester, New York, where the concept of combined team patrols was utilised (indicating a closer working relationship between response officers and detectives). This approach appeared to be more effective in relation to burglaries, robberies and thefts. That said, the criterion for effectiveness is important, because, while arrests increased significantly, clearances and convictions did not, indicating enthusiasm of teams to do a good job, but little discerning behaviour in the quality of arrests.

Exploring the variety of investigative roles within law enforcement departments in the USA, Repetto identified five different types of investigators. He distinguished them based on the nature of their roles (i.e. local or national investigator, proactive or reactive, or by the seriousness of the crimes they investigated), or the nature of the training they received to undertake them. Repetto distinguished them according to whether they utilised art, craft or science within their investigations. Repetto drew on a study by Wilson (1978) relating to the work of both FBI and DEA agents. The five roles incorporated: regional or national level detectives dealing with crimes of high-level significance usually on a reactive basis (see Wilson, 1978, for instance, in relation to the work of the FBI; detectives engaged in local-level crime investigations (working primarily reactively); intelligence officers or analysts; administrative detectives (those preparing cases post-arrest or occasionally conducting local crime patrol duties); and undercover police officers (or 'instigators') working proactively (see Wilson, 1978 for a description of the work of the DEA). Repetto (1978) criticised RAND for ignoring the subtle differences between these different roles and the different skills required in order to perform them effectively.

According to Repetto (1978), investigators working at regional or national level represented the closest to the scientific dimension (as opposed to art and craft). He justified this on the basis that they were skilled operatives recruited from the ranks of highly educated people and subjected to rigorous training. Investigators working at a lower level (including intelligence officers or analysts) were more reflective of the craft dimension. Repetto argued that they were not recruited on the basis of their level of education, and thus represented a diverse educational entity. They were usually drawn from the ranks of uniformed police officers deemed suitable because of their street experience. These officers traditionally learnt 'on the job' through experience, peer learning, and training to complement their development (Repetto, 1978; Hobbs, 1988; Innes, 2003). Undercover operatives, according to Repetto, utilised skills from the art dimension. Repetto's work served to reinvigorate the discussion over the categorisation of detective work into the dimensions of art, craft and science, although he gave little assistance in relation to the nature and type of skills involved. Wilson (1978) provides some discussion of the art dimension, suggesting that DEA agents required particular manipulative skills to persuade people to engage in criminality, particularly when they were undertaking undercover activities, and artful skills to be able to gain reliable information to assist their investigations.

Tong and Bowling (2006) preferred to see the art, craft and science dimensions as stereotypes not representing reality or a stark choice between them. They argued that the art and craft dimensions tend to accentuate the perception that experience is paramount, and that learning on the job is above any other form of education because the art and craft cannot be found outside of the reality and practice of investigation. Such thinking is likely to perceive the good investigator as an individualistic, mystical figure and perpetuate myths and stereotypes about investigative skill, training and education. It is also likely to instil the idea that minimal training and professional development is required as the learning is all internal to the practitioner, based on their unique experiences. In these dimensions, the idea of accountability suffers because there is no standard by which to judge the professional practice. Any standard is internalised and not open to external scrutiny. Tong and Bowling (2006) suggest that the science dimension involves a more systematic and methodical approach to investigations: the individualistic mythical investigator gives way to an investigator utilising scientific principles that are clearly articulated and understood, and that stand as minimum standards applied to modern investigators and their investigations. These principles are capable of being taught, in contrast to the arts and crafts. It is important to note, however, that the authors do suggest that as the dimensions are fluid, practice is likely to engage a combination of all three.

Recent UK studies have tended to support this notion (Innes, 2003; O'Neill, 2011). Innes found that homicide detectives considered their work to employ all three dimensions. O'Neill (2011) conducted research on volume crime investigators in six sites across EW. In relation to whether investigative work could be characterised as an art, craft, science or a mixture of all three dimensions, 64 respondents (investigators in volume crime teams ranging from constable to Inspector) were asked to consider how investigation could be characterised. A majority (62%) considered that investigation was a mixture of all three dimensions. Investigation was considered to be solely an art by 7.8%, a craft by 3.12% and a science by 6.25%. A number (13%) felt that it was something other than the above choices. The majority of people who fell into the 'other' bracket identified investigation as being a mixture of craft and science. The respondents were not, however, asked to identify what particular aspects of their practice encompassed any of the dimensions.

None of these studies provide a detailed insight into what skills, attributes or features inhabit each dimension (Westera et al, 2014). Similarly, there appear to be few that have deconstructed investigative practice to the extent that one can discern a list of qualities and skills that make for effective practice (Westera et al, 2014). Effective communication has often been cited as crucial (Wilson, 1978; Cohen and Chaiken, 1987; McGurk et al, 1992; Maguire et al, 1992; O'Neill and Milne, 2014), but even this concept has only recently seen attempts to define it in the investigative sphere. Westera et al, 2014, conducted a small scale study with 30 detectives in Australia and New Zealand, in order to define some of the common skills abilities or characteristics identified by previous research as central to effectiveness (decision-making, communication, motivation, leadership, etc.). The authors derived definitions for some of these key areas. For example, respondents described communication in terms of being able to (among other things) communicate through a variety means, to different kinds of people, establishing rapport and a relationship of trust, demonstrating empathy and being non-judgemental (Westera et al, 2014, p 10).

This type of definition provides a useful starting point for consideration, while at the same time raising more questions about the characteristics required to be able to *effectively* gain rapport, to *effectively* demonstrate empathy, or *effectively* establish a relationship of trust. It is one thing to know what is necessary, but putting it into practice is another. Westera et al, 2014 suggest that further research is needed to define other skills. A catalogue of skills would provide a useful starting point to assess what skills (if any) sit within the dimensions of art, craft or science when put into practice. This is particularly important so that areas once thought of as innate qualities can be more rigorously assessed (see the discussion below, for instance, in relation to intuition and its relationship to acute observation). Indeed, further research in these areas could enable a better understanding of investigative practice. The following sections will briefly consider what facets may occupy each of the art, craft and science dimensions.

The art dimension

Wilson (1978) suggested that art, in the context of proactive undercover police officers, included the ability to extract information and the ability to manipulate others into committing crime. Apart from the ethical minefield involved in the second example, others have added to that list, suggesting that it also encompasses creativity, intuition, flair and imagination (Tong and Bowling, 2006). Aligned to these artistic notions is the assumption that individuals have innate qualities to perform their role. As such, these qualities cannot be taught – they are either present or they are not. Such artists do not necessarily utilise methodical approaches, but tend to use their insight and imagination to solve cases. What is interesting about this analogy is that it appears to be fuelled by both fiction (in the form of detective stories, and by the tales of 'derring do' by detectives themselves (Shpayer-Makov, 2011). One has to be naturally sceptical of detective memoirs, first on the basis of the potential for personal aggrandisement and second for the potential for cases to be 'sexed-up' for public consumption. Either way, such publications cannot be said to reflect reality. This is not to suggest that there have never been cases where investigators have used artistic qualities to solve cases. It is simply to identify that there is no known research on solved cases where artistic qualities have been the sole reason for success.

Creativity within investigations has received some attention within academic research, most notably by Dean et al (2008). They undertook research into the different decision-making styles of Norwegian SIOs, and explored the concept of creativity in decision-making. Defining creativity as 'behaviours and activities that are directed at developing novel solutions that work for the investigation' (Dean et al, 2008, p 176), the authors suggested that it could involve both flair and imagination. They conceptualised four thinking styles engaged by detectives in homicide investigations. These were skill style, risk style, method style and challenge style. While creativity formed part of each of the four styles, SIOs appeared to utilise creativity more within the risk and skill styles, particularly when an investigation was at a stage where new strategies and leads were required to continue momentum because other strategies and actions had proved fruitless. Dean et al (2008) also noticed that risk and skill styles were typical of experienced practitioners, an observation that led them to suggest that creativity may also be linked to the craft dimension, where experience tends to have influence on expert practice.

Recently, Fox (2014) undertook a study of SIOs in both the UK and the USA. Responses suggested that SIOs in the UK considered that their flair, imagination and creativity was being stifled by guidance and policy on investigations, to the point that they felt obliged to undertake investigations routinely. Such routinisation, they suggested, stifled the natural creativity of practitioners who felt compelled to undertake routine practices merely to cover themselves if things went wrong. Major crime investigations are guided by doctrines such as the MIM (ACPO, 2006) and MIRSAP (ACPO, 2005), much of which has been derived from practitioners. Indeed, MIRSAP and the use of the Home Office Large Major Enquiry System (HOLMES) specifically evolved from lessons learnt from the flawed Yorkshire Ripper investigation in the 1980s (Byford, 1981), and the Lawrence investigation (Macpherson, 1999). MIM and MIRSAP provide guidance to investigators on all aspects of major crime investigation. Whilst guidance is not mandatory, one could argue that because of their entrenched nature in investigative practice, it would be a foolhardy SIO who departs from them without good reason. That said, SIOs can choose strategies and actions to utilise, and, as lead investigators, are able to make decisions on which they are ultimately accountable. Creativity, imagination and flair appear to be possible within this structure. Indeed, CD encourages the use of creativity, especially when other investigative avenues have been explored to no avail. The SIOs in Fox's study do not describe the creative practices they cannot use within the constraints of MIM and MIRSAP. This would have been useful, particularly when creativity is identified by Smith and Flanagan (2000) as an important SIO skill. Wright (2013) reports that SIOs feel that their role has moved from an investigative one to a more managerial one with a consequent stifling of intuition, particularly in the early stages of a major crime investigation.

CD does not reject the use of intuition, suggesting that it can be useful in appropriate circumstances, although Fahsing and Ask (2013) note the negative language within CD that discourages its use. Academics have suggested that hunches and gut feeling have a place in investigations, providing they are recorded appropriately (Savage and Milne, 2007). While CD appears less than positive towards the use of some of these artistic qualities, there is little detailed discussion or clear definition of terminology. Nor is there a discussion of their advantages and disadvantages when employed within investigations, and what research has to say (if anything) about each of them. While there is some material on heuristics and biases in CD, this appears lacking when one considers the importance of decision-making to criminal investigations (for a fuller discussion of investigative decision-making, see Chapter 4).

Intuitive thinking is often used by humans in fast-paced situations where decisions are required on the spot. While such decisions can be accurate, linked as they are to fight-or-flight mechanisms, they are prone to error (Tversky and Kahneman, 1974). Kahneman (2011) describes intuitive decisions as system one thinking. He also describes system two thinking, which is deployed in slower time, and is more rational, where the decision-maker has more time to weigh up competing possibilities. According to Kahneman (2011) system two thinking is less prone to error. System one thinking is likely to be employed by police officers when they are responding to emergency situations, whereas system two thinking is more likely to be most effective in the context of post- or pre-event criminal investigations, providing it is utilised appropriately. As such, it is important that it is given primacy in detective training and education.

Some commentators suggest that intuition is more likely to be acute observational skills (Rossomo, 2008; Wright, 2013; O'Neill, in press), while others consider it central to the detective's inferential thinking and hypothesis development (Wright, 2013). Describing intuition as 'the ability to automatically go beyond the information available to develop hypotheses and make inferences' (Wright, 2013, p 183), Wright conducted research with 40 UK homicide detectives of varying ranks and experience (mean 18 years' service as detectives). Over half (28) were experienced SIOs. Participants were asked to sort crime scenes into different categories of their own making, but while doing so to describe their decision aloud. In debrief, detectives were asked to explain their thought processes. Detectives made 594 inferences and were accurate in 398 (67%) of them. Higher-ranking detectives generated a larger number of inferences from crime scenes than lower-ranking officers. Wright (2013) concluded that the ability to generate hypotheses was linked to investigator knowledge and experience (potentially the craft), although these findings appear at odds with the research of Fahsing and Ask (2016), who found that experienced

Norwegian detectives fared no better than less-experienced police officers and students in this regard, although UK detectives fared better than less-experienced police officers and staff.

The craft dimension

There is a potential overlap between facets described in the art domain and the craft domain, but craft is dominated by the idea that experience and time spent as investigator is superior to book learning and science (Hobbs, 1988; Chatterton, 1995; Innes, 2003; O'Neill, in press). Using guile and common sense are facets of this domain (Wilson, 1978). While classically considered to be part of the detective psyche, many of the same views of effective policing are reflected in the general rank and file, in what Sherman calls the smothering paradigm (Sherman, 2015). This connotes a stubborn resistance to anything alien to the concept of craft dominance, such as science, education and training. In relation to criminal investigation, the craft mentality is fuelled and supported by fictional portrayals of detectives as hard-bitten experienced detectives with knowledge of the world (a good example is the portrayal of the English TV detective, Inspector Frost). Despite experience being considered core to craft, Fahsing and Ask (2016) found that experience was insufficient to guarantee professional competence. Experienced Norwegian SIOs were compared with non-experienced police and civilians in relation to a series of serious crime vignettes. The same process was undertaken with SIOs in the UK. While the experienced UK detectives performed better than the other groups, the experienced Norwegian detectives fared less well, even against inexperienced Norwegian officers. Fahsing and Ask (2016) suggested that the most obvious difference between the experienced detectives from each country was the process of development of SIOs. SIOs in the UK (since 2005) were the product of the PIP development process, whereas Norwegian detectives had no similar developmental programme. The authors proposed that the development of SIOs in Norway could be enhanced by a process similar to PIP. In O'Neill's study of volume crime investigators (2011), investigators asked to rate 30 skills, abilities and characteristics required to be a successful investigator rated communication, motivation, commitment, dedication, initiative and decision-making as very important. All of these facets were ranked quite important or very important by at least 90% of respondents. In contrast, in the areas of education, strategic awareness, training, empathy and leadership, over 50% of respondents felt they were moderately important or lower. Training and education were ranked low (training 27th, education 30th). Interestingly, experience was also ranked low (22nd out of 30), suggesting that respondents were not wedded to the notion of experience as key, despite being negative towards training and education.

The science dimension

The science dimension is multi-faceted. Four aspects will be considered here:

- classic science as an aid to investigations;
- science used to inform crime management practices;
- science in terms of the manner in which it informs investigative practice; and
- science used to inform investigative decision-making.

Classic science as an aid to investigations

Science in the classic sense connotes the use made of it to assist proof within criminal investigations. It can also be used to eliminate suspects. Apart from the use of forensic science, engaging aspects of biology, chemistry and physics (Stelfox, 2009), scientific advances in the field of both fingerprints and DNA have significantly improved the capacity of the police to solve crimes, assuming there are sufficient resources and the wherewithal to be able to successfully gather it at actual or potential crime scenes. Sometimes, fingerprints and DNA can provide direct proof of guilt, but often their presence amounts to circumstantial evidence with a requirement for the police to prove more.

Fingerprints and DNA have been credited with heralding a new scientific era in investigation. Police investigators must be aware of these fruitful avenues, and must marshal resources and assimilate the results of those activities within their investigations (Stelfox, 2009). While the harnessing of science has grown, commentators such as Innes (2010) provide a cautionary note as to its usefulness. There are cases that would never have been solved without the use of scientific methods. However, there are investigations that do not yield forensic evidence at all. Innes (2010) points out that scientific advancements do not solve cases on their own. Sometimes there is no forensic evidence at a scene. In any investigation, science is only one of a number of strategies utilised. Innes (2010) suggests that sometimes the increased use of science within policing leads to detrimental effects. The lack of fingerprints or DNA, for example, could produce lazy investigations, where the absence of scientific proof could be seen as the end to an investigation. Cases such as Levi Bellfield's 2011 conviction for the murder of Amanda 'Milly' Dowler did not rely on forensic evidence, but a careful and thorough re-evaluation of the evidence in the case, taking care to detail the pattern of Bellfield's offending before, during and after his previous offences. It is suggested that this kind of case re-evaluation is rare compared to limited cold-case reviews designed to ascertain whether new forensic opportunities exist. Of course, fingerprint evidence, DNA, and other scientific methods also allow those suspected of crimes to be eliminated from investigations, and those wrongfully convicted to be set free (for instance, the case of Pitchfork, where DNA exonerated a person who falsely confessed to a rape and murder: see Wambaugh, 2011). More recently, Ludwig and Fraser (2014) traced over 30 years of research, government reports and policy documents to conclude that the use of science within volume crime investigations was still hampered by a lack of standardisation, knowledge and training. Therefore, despite the promise of science, more could be done to use it to its full potential.

Science used to inform and influence crime management practices

Crime management principles and practices evolved from studies such as RAND (Greenwood et al, 1977; Bottomley and Coleman, 1981). Screening processes have evolved to make efficient and effective use of police resources, and crime management systems and processes evolved in the UK to support National Intelligence Model (NIM) protocols (James, 2016). The Volume Crime Investigation Manual (VCIM) (ACPO, 2001) and its accompanying Volume Crime Management Model (VCMM) (ACPO, 2009a), for instance, encourage a strategic response to crimes considered to be priority, and NIM systems and processes are utilised (i.e. strategic management, intelligence profiles, tactical responses, minimum standards for initial response) to ensure that identified crimes are responded to appropriately (James, 2016). Cases are most likely to be solved when there is a professional response, good scene management, together with effective questioning that contributes towards identifying evidential opportunities. Strategic management processes described here attempt to improve effectiveness through focussed responses. Crime screening processes now screen out a significant number of cases, meaning that a percentage of cases receive little or no investigative attention (other than the initial screening). Recent research by James and Mills (2012) suggests that this practice is being expanded, in austerity, to enable the police service to cope with extreme demand. All against the backdrop of the latest critique of the police response to criminal investigations (HMIC, 2017). Police were criticised for filing cases without a proper investigation having been undertaken, arresting fewer people, and failing to capture those wanted in connection with criminal offences.

Science used to inform investigative practice

In the area of investigative interviewing, much has been learnt from the field of psychology (Williamson, 2007). Following a litany of miscarriages of justice between the 1970s and early 1990s, there were perceptible efforts by the police service to improve this area of practice (Baldwin, 1992; Baldwin, 1993; Savage and Milne, 2007; Williamson, 2007). Much research has underpinned the development of both suspect and witness interviewing, with flexible frameworks developed to assist investigators in both planning and executing interviews in different settings (Bull, 2014; Shepherd and Griffiths, 2013). The importance of communication to the process of interviewing has also been well documented. The PEACE model, the Cognitive Interview, and the Enhanced Cognitive Interview, have all been developed through psychological research to improve the range of investigative interview practices, although there is still room for further improvement (Clarke and Milne, 2001; Clarke et al, 2011; Bull, 2014). Further studies are continuing in relation to the best style to utilise when interviewing suspects for murder and sexual offences (Oxburgh, 2015).

Research was also undertaken into eyewitness testimony. This has informed the way that police practice has evolved, not only in interview, but in the procedural aspects of identification processes. Due to the unreliable nature of eyewitness testimony, identified by numerous studies (Williamson, 2007), and because of high-profile miscarriages of justice linked to the issue (Devlin, 1976), the PACE Codes of Practice include sections specifically designed to safeguard suspects' rights with regard to identification issues (Code D). The classic legal case of R v Turnbull (1977) if followed, ensures that fundamental detail is secured from witnesses in order to assist judgements later relating to witness credibility and reliability. Despite the influence of research on this area, however, practice will always be variable, because where human interaction takes place, the coincidence of knowledge, application, decision-making, emotion, prejudice, discrimination and other factors will all play a part to determine the outcome.

The application of the scientific method to investigative decision-making

It is striking that the police service has failed to provide a clear decision-making model for criminal investigations, although it could be argued that the new National Decision Model (NDM) does exactly that (see Chapter 4). CD describes the typical stages of a criminal investigation without clearly articulating *how* investigators should think. While suggesting that officers should employ an investigative mindset, the ABC of crime and hypothesis testing, CD does not provide either a structure or sufficient practical guidance to enable officers to perform the task. The original version of CD encouraged investigators to keep an open mind, presumably as a counter to the raft of miscarriage of justice cases that demonstrated that this had not occurred in the past (Irving and Dunnighan, 1993; ACPO, Centrex, 2005; Savage and Milne, 2007; Stelfox, 2009). It suggested that investigators develop an 'investigative mindset', contending that hypotheses may be utilised in certain circumstances. However, CD failed to provide any real guidance on the decision-making process, and adopted a negative approach to hypothesis formulation and testing (Tong et al, 2009). This, despite the fact that, as a matter of human nature, investigators formulate hypotheses from the moment they attend a crime scene (Wright, 2013). CD spends little time on cognitive biases, despite the importance of understanding their power in the process of investigation (Stelfox and Pease, 2005). Indeed, CD gave scant regard to decision-making, bearing in mind its importance to MOJs (Bryant, 2009b). Innes (2003) identified different types of thinking styles for homicide detectives, but these were, according to him, all undertaken using the process of abduction. This was observed by Innes (2003) as happening naturally in the way that investigators reasoned about murder investigations. In this process (reasoning to the best explanation), hypotheses are formulated and tested, refuted or accepted based on the information that enters an investigation (Carson, 2007; 2009a). Any hypothetico-deductive approach would need to be clearly articulated in order for practitioners to utilise it appropriately. CD appears to suggest some of these approaches without any explanation as to how they combine within an investigation. While Stelfox (2009) notes the iterative nature of a more complicated investigation, without the golden thread of hypothetico-deductive thinking, investigations are in danger of being conducted in the same manner as investigations prior to the inception of PIP. That is, sometimes blinkered, assumptive and lacking in objectivity. Chapter 4 considers the issue of investigative decision-making in further detail.

Having considered the separate dimensions of art, craft and science as they relate to criminal investigation, it is important to acknowledge that these ideal types were formulated prior to the inception of the professionalisation agenda in the UK. It could be reasoned that, bearing in mind this backdrop, efforts would be made in the new paradigm to assert the prevalence of the scientific investigator, albeit recognising that the art and craft dimensions would naturally play some part (West, 2001; Phillips, 2002; Innes, 2003; O'Neill, 2011). Figure 2.1 demonstrates the posited shift in emphasis from the historical dominance of art and craft towards the dominance of science in the senses described above. Any shift is yet to be empirically proven, although whatever the dominant domain, craft will always be central, and this is reflected by the circle in Figure 2.1.

It is useful to reflect on the three dimensions, and whether they represent sufficiently robust interpretations of practice to be able to form a separate dimension of Figure 1.2 (posited in Chapter 1). If that were the case, investigations could be suspect-centred, event-centred or hybrid (domain one), volume series or major (domain two), art-, craft- or science-oriented (domain three), and proactive, reactive, and hybrid (domain four). Depending on its focus, any investigation could contain at least one facet from each domain, and potentially could fluctuate between a number in each domain as it progresses. As such, Brodeur's ten types of criminal investigation could be multiplied even further. Such an analysis tends to underline the complexity of criminal investigation work and the problem with attempts to define it (see Appendix, Figure A.1).

Gundhus (2012) provides an interesting discussion of the nature of change and professionalisation. Drawing on empirical research of attempts to utilise knowledge-based policing in Norway, Gundhus suggests two different perspectives in relation to the term 'professionalism'. On the one hand, experience-based perceptions accentuate the importance of individuality, subjectivity, gut feeling and instinct, while the standardised perception exemplifies formal competence, standards and the use of technology. Seen in this way, one could suggest that with the advent of PIP, the impact of new standards of investigations, and the increased use of technology to combat modern forms of criminality, there is a shift from art towards science, and thus inexorably towards professionalisation. However, Gundhus (2012) found cultural negativity towards the new evidence-based paradigm with low status accorded to theoretical knowledge and high status still afforded by practitioners to experience.

Figure 2.1: The shift from art towards science

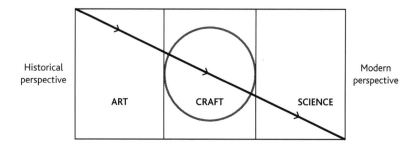

While some steps have been taken towards professionalising the investigative role, particularly in relation to structured professional development of investigators (McGrory and Treacy, 2012), questions still remain about the difference between the rhetoric and the reality. Chapter 3 will further detail the development of investigators under the auspices of PIP. However, any development of investigative practice thus far needs to be seen in the context of government austerity measures since 2011. Can the rhetoric of professionalisation withstand the challenges of police forces required to tailor their responses according to budgetary constraints and a streamlined workforce? While there are few studies on the direct effects of austerity on investigations in the UK, there are a number that can shed light on potential issues.

Austerity

In October 2010, the Government announced its Spending Review. In response to the financial downturn, the government committed to apply austerity measures designed to rescue a poor financial situation left (in their opinion) by the outgoing Labour Government (Loveday, 2015). Some commentators suggest a more deep-seated political agenda, favouring deregulation and privatisation of state functions (Brogden and Ellison, 2013). Others argue that the real reason for police reform (under the auspices of austerity) lay in the need to change an organisation that did not represent value for money and one that was proving ineffective in relation to the crime problem (Loveday, 2015). This last point is supported by figures for police pay, overtime claims, and ancillary expenditure arguably signposting financial wastage (Mills et al, 2010; Brogden and Ellison, 2013). The police were subject to a 20% cut from central government funding during the period 2011/12 to 2014/15 (HMIC, 2011). According to the HMIC, workforce reductions were expected to relate to over 16,000 police officers,

1,800 PCSOs, and 16,000 civilian staff. This figure has recently risen to 20,000 police officers and over 6,000 PCSOs. Opposition by the Police Federation was considered ineffective (Brogden and Ellison, 2013). While assessing the true depth of the cuts is difficult, early proposals suggested that civilian staff, call handling units, control room staff, witness care units, scientific support staff, and roads policing would be first casualties (Brogden and Ellison, 2013). Force collaborations, outsourcing of key functions, better procurement and contractual arrangements with third parties, and an increased reliance on volunteers were all identified as pathways to better efficiency (HMIC, 2014a). While these measures might achieve some cost benefits (Caswell, 2014), Loveday (2008, 2015) suggests that they have superseded workforce modernisation initiatives where efficiency and effectiveness have proven possible, even in the sphere of criminal investigation (for instance, the Mixed Economy Teams (MET), constituting both civilian and police investigators). Cost efficiency also led commentators to question whether *other* perceived luxuries might be vulnerable to cuts. Without Home Office funding for instance, would cold-case reviews of major crime cases survive the cuts (Allsop, 2013)?

Home Secretary Theresa May and Police Minister Nick Herbert stated in 2011 that frontline services would be protected. However, the term 'frontline' was ill-defined in political rhetoric, the Home Office, and within policing circles in EW (Hughes, 2011) (The term was eventually clarified by the HMIC following consultation [HMIC, 2011]). Brogden and Ellison (2013) note that there was an underlying assumption that privatisation of backroom functions would lead to more frontline staff. They considered the effects of some early changes, where civilian staff were replaced by expensive police officers untrained to undertake the role they were asked to fulfil. Far from freeing officers for frontline roles, austerity had the opposite effect (Brogden and Ellison, 2013). Turnbull and Wass (2015) conducted research into the effects of austerity on 'extreme work' undertaken by police inspectors. They characterised extreme work as having any five of ten characteristics. These included many facets of police work, not necessarily restricted to the rank of inspector. For example, presence in the workplace at least ten hours daily, fast-paced work with mandatory deadlines, unpredictable work, responsibility commensurate with more than one role, large amounts of travel, accountability and availability to the public, work-related activities outside usual hours, responsibility for profit and loss, and responsibility for staff development and recruitment. They noted how police inspectors were tending to work far longer hours due to budget constraints and demand for more officers. The idea of 'doing more with less' was reported to be having a profound effect on the amount of work expected of an inspector. Detective inspectors suggested that their workload was even higher. The worrying aspect of these working practices is that they appear to be expected, even encouraged. They resonate with police culture – officers wanting to do a good job regardless of the consequences in terms of longer hours and potential for ill health. One respondent noted how the police were good at supporting officers following a traumatic incident at work, but almost absent when staff were suffering due to high workload. The research found that, pre-austerity, inspectors worked on average 44 hours per week, while post-austerity, the figure rose to 48. But what support and understanding was available if officers either suffered sickness through stress or made mistakes due to heavy workload? When asked at a police conference whether an inspector would be able to plead austerity as a defence to making a mistake on a review of a mentally ill prisoner, Chief Inspector of Constabulary Tom Winsor reportedly stated that there would be no excuse, as the liberty of any suspect was too important to get wrong (Brogden and Ellison, 2013).

Both Brogden and Ellison (2013) and Turnbull and Wass (2015) suggest that in austerity, police discipline has been utilised to ensure that more for less is achieved from current police employees (both civilian and officer roles). However, they ask the question: at what cost? A recent *Guardian* newspaper article (2016) identified that police sickness for psychological reasons rose significantly in five years, rising from 19,825 in 2010/11 to 22,547 in 2014/15 (Hargreaves et al, 2016). On 31 March 2016, it was reported that 2,249 officers were long-term sick, an increase of 11.5% on the previous year (Home Office, 2016).

In 2014, the Police Federation of EW commissioned research into police morale in austerity. An online questionnaire was conducted, with over 13,000 officers responding. The questionnaire contained a mixture of qualitative and quantitative questions, and data analysis was undertaken. The authors noted that they conducted statistical analysis to ascertain whether there were any skewing effects from either geographical or rank difference. They found no statistical differences (Hoggett et al, 2014). It is not possible to reproduce all the results here. However, a number of findings are particularly relevant to any discussion of the effects of austerity. Results must be seen in the context of a workforce affected not only by budgetary constraints affecting service provision, but in relation to the 2012 Winsor review of pensions, pay and conditions (Rogers and Gravelle, 2012). In response to questions relating to the relationship between police and government, 88.5% of respondents disagreed or strongly disagreed with the statement that cuts would not impact on their ability to do the job. Moreover, 78.1% either disagreed or strongly disagreed that they had the resources to do their job. Finally, 97.8% either disagreed or strongly disagreed that cuts to policing would not affect service resilience. One respondent suggested: 'There are not enough resources to do our job effectively and so we are providing the public with poor service' (Hoggett et al, 2014, p 51). A worrying picture can also be discerned from the following quote from a respondent:

> The workload has increased dramatically as there are less officers to investigate crime, attend incidents, obtain evidence, when the number of assignments has not in any way decreased. This in turn is leading to more sickness through stress and depression, as officers are struggling to cope with the burdens, and that means there are even less officers available when people are either absent or restricted duties because of sickness. And this inevitably is severely affecting our ability to do the job the public expects of us. (Hoggett et al, 2014, pp 53–4)

While this research is arguably partisan, commissioned as it was by the Police Federation, the authors point out that it was subject to a rigorous methodological approach, and had to receive ethical approval through a university ethics committee. Moreover, there are similarities in this study with another report on detectives in 2008. Chatterton (2008) found dissatisfaction among general office CID (GOCID) investigators (that is, CID officers who deal with serious and complex crime on a local level), with lack of resourcing of the department and a general loss of skills to specialist departments and a perceived lack of support for detective work. This pre-austerity study (also undertaken on behalf of the Police Federation), produced a bleak picture of lack of staffing of GOCID and consequent issues that practitioners had in relation to service to the public and morale. This led Chatterton (2008) to assert that there was a serious morale issue, inasmuch as detectives felt that their work was being undervalued, progression through the PIP process was given lip service, with training and development ignored at the expense of 'getting the job done'. Additionally, many felt that more effort was put into clearing minor crime (easy cases) at the expense of real crime (more serious and complex). While chasing easy clear-ups had the potential to appease the public, Chatterton warned that it also had the effect of criminalising undeserving members of the public, leaving real criminals to pursue their criminal activities. This could have an effect on officer morale, especially if they perceive they are not given the opportunity to utilise their skills, except on the least demanding of investigations. This study seemed to indicate a lack of resource dedicated to GOCID even before austerity, and there are limited studies of the effects of austerity on the provision of investigative services (James and Mills, 2012). That said, the G4S and Lincolnshire Police partnership experiment demonstrates that post-austerity forces looked for a more cost-effective way of dealing with policing functions (Rogers and Gravelle, 2012). While crime investigation per se was not on the agenda, the crime management bureau, the criminal justice unit and learning and development were part of the 18 service areas in the contract (White, 2014). In 2017, HMIC conducted a PEEL review of forces. They identified what they describe as a 'crisis point' in relation to a shortage of investigators nationally, leading to high workload and stress for those left in the roles. While the reason for the shortage has not been studied, Chatterton's 2008 study and the effects of austerity appear to be taking their toll. In 2017, the MPS began recruiting direct entry detectives with a structure of training that includes PIP levels one and two within the first two years of service, in effect, fast-tracking towards a detective career. Amid suggestions that the scheme could potentially create tensions between traditional officers and an elite group, the MPS recruitment drive has accentuated the support from existing detectives, although this is yet to be tested within an investigative culture notoriously conservative and insular (MPS, 2017).

Finally, the HMIC report demonstrates some unintended consequences of austerity. Police, unable to cope with demand for finite resources, have downgraded calls, reclassified risk and failed to classify organised crime groups appropriately. This, in addition to failing to thoroughly investigate lower-level crimes, arresting fewer people and failing to capture those wanted on warrant (HMIC, 2017). The picture painted by HMIC is against the backdrop of significant cuts, yet the report implies that the police are not using their resources effectively. According to HMIC, of 43 forces, 13 required improvement, while one was labelled 'inadequate'.

Conclusion

This chapter has briefly explored the historical development of detective work in terms of a trajectory away from the art and craft of investigative work towards a new scientific professional practice. Rhetoric suggests that there is a shift in emphasis, and that this is accompanied by more professional investigations, thereby providing a better service to the public. Yet, while science has been embraced in some senses, some old cultural values remain. The craft mentality remains dominant still, recently supported by a CoP announcement concerning the development of investigators on a craft-like basis, absent training provision and with a greater accent on workplace learning (O'Neill, in press). This appears to be a pragmatic response to austerity rather than a real embracing of professionalisation. Even though craft dominates, evidence-based policing promises a strong partnership with research that informs professional practice. This could preserve the centrality of craft while concentrating research efforts on enhancing investigative knowledge. There is an opportunity to prioritise important aspects of practice, such as investigative decision-making. In that area, questions remain about the utility of the NDM to criminal investigations (this will be discussed in detail in Chapter 4). Even though the terms art, craft and science have excited debate in the past, there is still a lack of understanding of the skills, abilities or characteristics populating each domain, or indeed whether these terms are even relevant today. Current rhetoric would suggest that the police are coping well with government austerity measures, yet some studies lift the veil and give cause for concern. Lack of resources, poor morale, an increase in workload and increased sickness levels point to a different perspective on the ground. In the next chapter, investigative development via training will be explored and a further gap between rhetoric and reality discussed.

Further reading

Brogden, M. and Ellison, G. (2013) *Policing in an age of austerity: A post-colonial perspective*. Abingdon: Routledge.

Greenwood, P., Chaiken, J. and Petersilia, J. (1977) *The criminal investigation process*. Lexington, MA: D.C. Heath.

Westera, N.J., Kebbell, M., Milne, R. and Green, T. (2014) 'Towards a more effective detective'. *Policing and Society: An International Journal of Research and Policy*, 26(1): 1–17.

THREE

Training investigators

Introduction

The previous chapter discussed the development of detective practice towards professionalisation. Aligned to the PIP process, modern investigators must qualify through a process of knowledge acquisition, training and workplace competence, in order to be able to investigate crimes of any seriousness or complexity. Today, investigators have a wealth of information at their fingertips in the form of Authorised Professional Practice (APP), National Centre for Applied Learning Technologies (NCALT) and the Police National Legal database (PNLD). There are movements to ensure best practice within an evidence-based policing (EBP) paradigm. CoP was created in 2012 as a central feature of professionalisation, aiming to develop the knowledge base of policing, develop staff through training and education, and to ensure standards in policing (including investigations). Already, a new code of ethics has been produced (CoP, 2014a), together with a National Decision Making model (NDM) designed to ensure ethical decision-making by practitioners exercising professional discretion. The previous chapter briefly considered how such developments have been affected by government austerity measures, but in what ways does this rhetoric of professionalisation survive reality in the training and development of investigators? This chapter will trace the development of investigator training to the modern day. How has it taken heed of public inquiries, Royal Commissions, high-profile MOJs and failed cases? What research underpins investigative training, the PIP process and the qualification and competencies required of a detective?

Training detectives

In 1829, when the Metropolitan Police was created, the idea of using plain-clothed detectives to investigate crimes was not supported (Beattie, 2012). Public disquiet about plain-clothed spies meant that the old system of Bow Street runners (detectives in all but name) still existed alongside new police for a period of time. Policing was supported on the understanding that men wore uniforms to ensure visibility and to distance them from spies (Hobbs, 1988). Police activity concentrated on crime prevention rather than detection and punishment of offenders, although arguably successful detection practices support that overriding objective. Police officers were citizens in uniform, derived from the public, thus requiring minimal specialist abilities to perform their role (Beattie, 2012). Therefore, it was considered that police work involved tasks that any member of the public could perform (Stelfox, 2009). In 1834, Rowan and Mayne famously reported to Parliament that no special skills were required to investigate crime (Beattie, 2012).

By 1840, the first official detectives within the Metropolitan Police were appointed. How were the eight pioneers chosen? What particular skills and abilities did they possess? How were they selected to accomplish their task? Because the role was new, some of the first detectives were drawn from former Bow Street Runners, while others were chosen for seemingly having aptitude for the role. Seeds of the early system of detective recruitment can be seen here: detectives were chosen from successful thief-takers, experienced individuals with the ability to 'read and know men'. In short, people were chosen on the basis that they had perceived ability. It is easy to see how an art and craft logic emanates from this perspective (Beattie, 2012; Emsley and Shpayer-Makov, 2006; Shpayer-Makov, 2011). As Valentine (1935) suggests, one has to start somewhere, and the development of police practice is no different to the development of other professions, where art and craft are eventually superseded by science, but not before initial practitioners become reliant on learning by experience. The police service has been slow to extricate itself from the dominance of craft (Sherman, 2015).

Myths about detective work grew because there were so few detectives in those early days (Morris, 2007; Beattie, 2012). They would often work alone, accentuating the individualistic nature of the role, and could at any time be asked to assist in crime investigations throughout the country. This system of loaning out the 'big guns' for investigations also fuelled the myth of detective work as an art and a craft (Innes, 2003). Innes observes that this practice was not discontinued until the 1950s, although seeds of the same mentality are still evident today in cases such as the Madeleine McCann and Ben Needham investigations, both of which involved British detectives taking the lead in investigations abroad. Widespread publicity ensures that part of the mythical status of detectives still pervades.

Within the first 100 years of official detective work, there were peaks and troughs. Peaks in the sense of successful high-profile cases being solved (such as the murder of Lord Russell in 1840, and the first murder on a train in Hackney in 1864). Troughs in the sense of high-profile cases *not* solved (particularly the Jack the Ripper murders), as well as scandals (such as the Turf Fraud case in 1877 where several leading detectives were imprisoned for their part in crime; Morris, 2007; Beattie, 2012). The corruption case led to the setting-up of a Criminal Investigation Department (CID) to provide structure to management and supervision of detectives. Emsley (2009), describes three unpublished reports on detective work at that time, all of which demonstrated that senior officers were dismissive of the complexity of investigations and qualities required to undertake them. In providing evidence to an 1878 Committee, Commissioner Henderson described criminal investigation as 'humdrum work' requiring nothing more than 'ordinary skill and intelligence' (Henderson, cited by Emsley, 2009, p 89).

By 1900, elements of science were beginning to prove useful in assisting investigations (Ramsland, 2014). These advances assured that investigation of crime was no longer a matter of a lone sleuth engaged in fighting crime: it involved scientific principles aligned to a more methodical approach to crimes, crime scenes and victims. Investigations were becoming more complex. No national detective training existed, although there were ad hoc events for detectives. It was not until 1902 that the first detective training school opened (Hobbs, 1988). The lack of any structured, systematic and uniform detective training was brought to the attention of the Desborough Committee in 1919. Because of police strikes over pay and conditions, the Committee had convened to investigate and make recommendations for the future. The Committee heard evidence from officers throughout England, Wales and Scotland. The final report recommended detective development should be based on practical experience, following effective probationary training (Desborough, 1920, p 9).

This was ambiguous. It appeared to suggest that detectives needed no further training than their uniform counterparts, providing the basic system of training was good enough. The skills of detective work could be learned on the job. It supports the notion of detective work as craft, yet the same recommendation went on to suggest sending detectives to the Metropolitan Police Detective Training school. The training provided there comprised six weeks of classroom learning, plus practical sessions using a magic lantern. Interestingly, the legal training was provided by an inspector with good knowledge of the law (minutes of evidence provided to the Desborough Committee by ACC Basil Thomson of the Metropolitan Police, 1920). Thomson outlined the typical manner in which an individual 'qualified' to become a detective in the Metropolitan Police.

First, the potential detective was likely to have been in uniform for three to four years, becoming acquainted with policing matters. At some point, the officer would have been involved in winter patrols, set up to combat local dwelling burglaries. As Thomson remarks, this was seen as a good training ground for fledgling detectives. Following that, officers would undergo a six-month probationary period. A six-week detective training event would follow, during which recruits would receive instruction in law, evidence and procedure and be tested on observational skills. A final examination would ensue (Desborough, 1920). The Desborough Committee, while seeing advantages in detective training, stopped short of recommending that it be mandatory. Tong et al (2009) argue that a consistent negative theme around detective work has been the assumption that detective work can only be learnt practically in the workplace, ignoring the potential for learning and education elsewhere. Thomson's evidence to the Desborough Committee supports the idea that the training element, while considered useful, was minimal compared to workplace experience. Brodeur and Dupont (2006), suggested policing accentuates *action* rather than reflection, and this is evident in training and research. It is not surprising therefore that reflection, education and training have been accorded second-order classification, below 'doing the job'.

The Departmental Committee on the Police (1938) identified the importance of scientific advancements in the investigation of crime. The committee, following a five-year study of detective work, recommended use of a scientific guide by all police officers, as well as more detailed training on criminal investigation to all officers (Moore and Rubin, 2014). Almost immediately, material was added to the uniform training syllabus, and detective training was available in various parts of the country in the form of eight-week courses for detective constables and six weeks for detective sergeants (Hobbs, 1988; Williamson et al, 2007; Moore and Rubin, 2014). Moore and Rubin (2014) note how the uniform syllabus contained criminal investigation matters, 60% of which related to investigative techniques, and 30% legal and evidential definitions. The detective course was intended to contain practical and theoretical sessions, including material on how to deal with crime scenes, witnesses, identification parades, packaging of exhibits, and taking of fingerprints and casts. Additionally, there was an emphasis on good knowledge of the law and court procedures (Moore and Rubin, 2014). Interestingly, the Committee suggested that officers should benefit from the fruits of experience prior to undertaking criminal investigations (Moore and Rubin, 2014, p 3). This despite the fact that little was written down in the form of organisational learning in order for it to happen. The police service has been lauded for capturing organisational knowledge, but criticised for its failure to capture tacit knowledge-that is, the knowledge of experience (Stelfox, 2009). In this sense, the idea of MIM and CD capturing the experience of others for the benefit of practitioners of the future is a valid one.

By 1970, the detective course had grown to 13 weeks in length. Rather surprisingly, the course consisted of criminal law taught in the abstract, and special interest lectures. Unlike probationer courses that had attempted to utilise role-play in order to develop practitioners, the CID course did not do so. Neither did it teach detectives how to investigate or detect crime (Laurie, 1970). As a result of a number of high-profile MOJs, most notably the Confait murder in 1972 and subsequent inquiry into the conviction of three innocent youths, the Royal Commission on Criminal Procedure (RCCP) was set up (Fisher, 1977; Philips, 1982). Various studies were undertaken, some concentrating on the issue of confessions. The Commission made recommendations to enshrine a suspect's rights in legislation, as well as the setting-up of an independent body to prosecute crimes. Consequently, within a few years, the Police and Criminal Evidence Act 1984 (PACE) was in place and the Crown Prosecution Service was created (Bull, 2014). Little changed in the process and nature of detective training, other than the accent on significant pieces of legislation such as PACE and a focus on the interviewing of suspects. Each regional detective course lacked consistency (Irving and McKenzie, 1993). The regime of a 10-week course dominated. However, in 1987 ACPO recommended that crime training should have a standard national course (Irving and McKenzie, 1993). National Police Training (NPT) designed a detective training course (Tong, 2005). The 14-week course was delivered regionally, by police forces licensed by NPT. This way, officers trained as detectives throughout the country had a similar minimum grounding in law and practice. The system allowed for improved mutual aid between forces, as all detectives would be trained to the same standard. In addition, staff transferring to another police force had the same training as their counterparts, irrespective of where in the country they qualified. Inspection regimes were set up to ensure that consistent standards were achieved by training centres. As well as these changes, the fundamental nature of detective training shifted between the next two research studies reviewed. There was a move from didactic training to skills development through facilitation and student-centred learning (Irving and McKenzie, 1993).

Morgan's 1990 study focused on one police force in the UK, and aimed to discover how crimes were solved, and whether any improvements could be made to the system. Fifty-two police officers were involved in the study, undertaken in the form of group discussions and questionnaires. Morgan reported that a number of those responding were current or former detectives, and uniformed officers. Regrettably, there is no breakdown of the distribution of these officers to contextualise the representativeness of the sample. Respondents felt that crimes were solved by: information from victims, witnesses and the public; 'spade work'; local knowledge; communication of information; personal qualities of the detective; time to pursue investigations; and luck. According to respondents, personal skills required to detect crime were: an ability to communicate; being approachable; knowledge of the local area; patience, persistence, tenacity and objectivity; time to pursue enquiries; and gut feelings. The finding that communication was an essential skill has been replicated in other studies since, including in the UK (Maguire et al, 1992; Soukara et al, 2002; O'Neill and Milne, 2014; Westera et al, 2014). So too have findings that officers feel that tenacity and persistence are crucial (O'Neill and Milne, 2014; Westera et al, 2014).

Morgan (1990) also examined training material from uniformed and detective training courses at six regional training centres. He noted that they all appeared to follow the syllabus mandated by the Home Office. However, Morgan found the course to be dominated by the training of criminal law. Of the 300 50-minute sessions on the ten-week course, he found that 110 sessions related to law (around 35% of the course). Little time, according to Morgan, was given to detective skills. For example, interviewing had seven sessions, four of which related to practicals. This represented a mere 10% of the course. Morgan suggested that the dominance of law was due to two reasons. First, to assist the detective in determining whether an offence had been committed, and second, to assist the detective prosecuting cases in court. At that point in time, detectives sometimes prosecuted their own cases, although this practice was eventually phased out.

Despite the advent of PACE, designed to ensure protection of citizens' rights, within a decade of the Philips Royal Commission (1982), further MOJs prompted yet another Royal Commission. It was appointed in 1989 to examine the effectiveness of the criminal justice system in securing convictions of the guilty and acquittal of the innocent (Runciman, 1993). The Commission had two years to report its findings. A number of research projects were commissioned, to look into particular aspects of the criminal justice process (Runciman, 1993).

Researchers were asked to carry out their work within a limited time frame, and this, according to some, caused issues in relation to the depth and breadth of their enquiries, the methodologies utilised, and any subsequent claims made (Irving and Dunnighan, 1993; Irving and McKenzie, 1993, Maguire and Norris, 1992). That said, the research agenda provided useful insights into criminal investigation and criminal investigation training.

Irving and Dunnighan (1993) conducted research relating to criminal investigation. Because of their limited time constraints (they had 16 weeks to report their findings), Irving and Dunnighan decided to engage in case histories. They were able to collect 60 case histories in one police force. They described their research as an exploratory study. In fact, they described their work as somewhere between research and consultancy. According to the authors, CID work had remained essentially the same for over 50 years. They also highlighted a paucity of evidence relating to the skills, abilities and characteristics required to effectively perform the role of detective.

Maguire and Norris also conducted research for the RCCJ. They aimed to identify the different ways in which criminal investigations were undertaken at different levels of crime seriousness, to discover how investigations were supervised, to identify problems with existing practice and determine best practice where possible. The authors suggested that time pressure to return the completed research limited the scope of their inquiry. Rather than being able to conduct a detailed analysis of cases and materials, the authors observed that they could only produce a snapshot of practice. The research took place within three police force areas, two metropolitan forces, and a county police force. The research design encompassed interviews with 75 detectives at all ranks, examination of case files, examination of further documentary evidence, and observations (120 hours). Because of time constraints, the authors noted, they had limited time for fieldwork. That said, they were able to visit a wide variety of divisional CID offices, specialist squads, incident rooms, intelligence units and other specialist resources. In addition, they spent three days observing training courses. The authors made it clear that their study did not utilise methodologies that allowed them to statistically analyse data, but nevertheless suggested that their research uncovered some important issues not previously considered in the literature. As with Hobbs' study (1988), Maguire and Norris reported that much was gained from both formal and informal meetings and interviews with officers, creating a good understanding of not only working practices but also the prevailing culture. While formal interviews were recorded contemporaneously, informal meetings were not. These were written up from memory shortly afterwards. Maguire and Norris noted how the ten-week detective training course was dominated by teaching of criminal law and the rules of evidence. Rather than being taught in an objective fashion, there were suggestions that some sessions contained a more sinister accent, with law being used as a weapon to manipulate suspects (see Chapter 5 for further discussion). The authors discovered a lack of regard for ethical principles, and the issue of wrongful convictions received scant attention. Little was taught about management and supervision of investigations, with training slanted towards techniques. Maguire and Norris found that investigators attended CID courses some time after working as detectives, because of workplace pressure and senior officer decisions to delay attendance. This had the effect of officers attending courses feeling that they already knew the job, because of their experience in the role. This reinforced the craft mentality and the idea that investigative work is best learnt on the job. A formal course appeared to have little relevance to a detective other than as a means to an end of qualification.

Separate from the RCCJ, McGurk et al (1992) undertook a training needs analysis in relation to detectives. They aimed to produce a skills directory for detective trainers to assist the planning of detective training. The research utilised a Position Analysis Questionnaire (PAQ). This used job descriptions and phrases compiled from research of a number of different occupations. The phrases used, for instance, included 'dealing with the public` and 'dealing with people in strained situations'. Fifteen detectives from four different forces were surveyed. The questionnaire asked detectives to rate the difficulty, importance and frequency of investigative tasks. Respondents rated tasks in terms of relevance to detective work. As an example, 'dealing with the public' received a percentile score of 98. Detectives therefore felt that their work involved that activity to a greater extent than 98% of all other tasks. Other activities receiving high percentile scores were 'interviewing' (98), 'dealing with people in strained situations' (96), and 'tolerating frustrating situations' (91). Lower scores related to 'amount of training required' (83), 'observing the inside of building' (83), and 'engaging in non-job related social contact' (84).

Tong (2005) criticised the findings of McGurk et al (1992), contending that the items used were ambiguous and described little about the actual skills required of detectives. Another potential shortfall of the analysis was to utilise a PAQ. While (according to Tong, 2005) the phrases and tasks utilised in the PAQ were valid to some extent, they were imported from other occupations. It was surprising, for instance, that tasks such as paperwork or case file construction did not appear within the list of most relevant tasks. These are often highlighted by officers as some of their most significant reasons for lack of time to investigate more crimes. Such mundane work, including paperwork, is part and parcel of the detective working life (Greenwood et al, 1977; Ericson, 1993). Nowadays, cases are unlikely to succeed without a properly built evidential case put together by an investigator (Stelfox, 2009). While the study can be criticised, McGurk et al (1992) did obtain detectives views on personal characteristics required for detective work. The most identified areas were: coping with separation from family and home; working with people for their benefit; interpreting feelings, ideas and facts; empathy – seeing matters from another's viewpoint; tolerating/evaluating uncertain and conflicting information; influencing other people's behaviour ideas and opinions; and dealing with people. The study also provided a list of abilities required for detective work, which included: produce ideas; generate new solutions to problems; communicate ideas in a spoken or written format; select the most appropriate solution to specific problems; articulate ideas fluently; listen to what is said; and organise and unify disorganised information. Morgan (1990, p 43) had noted gaps in understanding of skills required for the role:

> The confusion and less than clear perception within the police service of what attributes or skills are required by police detectives illustrate how the training of police and police detectives has never addressed the fundamental question of what qualities are required to teach investigators and what further qualities are necessary for the training of police detectives.

Despite some of the research outlined here, arguably this is still the case, more than 25 years after Morgan made this statement. While the National Occupational Standards (NOS) attempted to define all roles and the minimum competence levels required to perform them, these too can have the tendency to reduce the work to the lowest common denominator (Tong et al, 2009).

Maguire et al (1992) also asked CID officers to define the special skills that characterise a good investigator. They received a variety of responses, most of which are similar to those described above. For example, their study identified that good detectives were thought to possess a complex set of personal qualities including intelligence, common sense, initiative, inquisitiveness, independent thought, commitment, persistence, ability to talk to people, and an innate ability such as a 'nose' for the job or 'thief-taking ability'. According to Maguire et al (1992), and consistent with Morgan's study (1990), the most frequently mentioned ability was communication. As well as identifying personal qualities, Maguire et al went on to list a set of (possibly) learned skills that detectives also felt contributed to being a good investigator. These were: knowledge of the law, local knowledge, communication skills, interview techniques, file construction skills, cultivating informants, presenting evidence, and the ability to recognise and extract relevant information from documents (Maguire et al, 1992).

While this 1992 study is undoubtedly useful, its findings also need to be viewed with caution. Its questionnaire was administered to only a relatively small number of detective officers (26). Much of the other data was reportedly gleaned from group discussions with detectives. Despite limitations, the resultant findings do provide a flavour of what detectives thought made a good detective. While it is from a relatively recent time period, the changes in investigative work in the UK since then are vast. Legislation, new policies and practices, as well as scientific developments, have all moved on in the modern era. Little is known about the nature of investigative work in the 21st century.

Returning to Morgan (1990), he criticised detective courses for not teaching new and emerging skills. He cited interrogation techniques and TICs (e.g. Bottomley and Coleman, 1981). Interrogation is a word that is anathema to modern practice, and TICs have since been accompanied by scandal and corrupt practices (Young, 1991; Reiner, 1998; Patrick, 2011b). While TICs are part of an investigator's range of options, in the modern era they must be managed. Today, scandals persist in relation to the integrity of TICs (IPCC, 2012b; Home Affairs Committee, 2013). This discussion demonstrates how the concept of 'evidence-based policing' is relative, contextual and paradigmatic. When Morgan made his suggestions in 1990, it was impossible to predict that within a matter of years the face of investigative interviewing would be changed (Milne and Bull, 1999; Bull, 2014), and perhaps less surprisingly that TICs would be used as a game-playing tactic (Patrick, 2011b). The PEACE model of investigative interviewing was developed (by harnessing psychological research), with an accent on information-gathering rather than manipulative confession-seeking techniques. The time had come to complement rights laws with a change in practice. There is some evidence that changes were positive (Clarke and Milne, 2001), although there is still room for improvement (Clarke et al, 2011). Interview training was strategically led, and is now subsumed into PIP to complement training at PIP levels one and two (see also Chapter 2 on science to inform practice).

Smith and Flanagan (2000) set out to try to establish what skills, abilities and personal characteristics an effective senior investigative officer (SIO) ought to possess. The principal role of an SIO is to investigate stranger rapes, murders and abductions. The researchers interviewed 40 officers from ten different forces. Thirty of the officers were working on major crime investigations at various levels, distributed across forces, which were chosen in order to give a representative range of characteristics across the country. When interviewed, respondents were asked to identify effective SIOs. Ten SIOs were identified in this manner and were then interviewed. This research identified the complexity of the SIO role, requiring a wide range of skills, abilities and personal characteristics. Smith and Flanagan identified 22 attributes required for SIOs to perform effectively. The 22 skills were organised into three clusters: Investigative ability; knowledge; and management skills. The findings of this research strongly suggest that effectiveness at SIO level demands a combination of all three areas. Among the 22 skills is managing communication, leadership, investigative competence and decision-making.

Professionalising the Investigative Process (PIP)

PIP was introduced by the National Police Improvement Agency (NPIA) in 2005, with the aim to improve investigative competence at every level of the police service (ACPO, Centrex, 2005; Stelfox, 2009; McGrory and Treacy, 2012; CoP, 2017b). PIP was aimed at moving away from the art craft paradigm towards a scientific paradigm (Stelfox, 2007; James and Mills, 2012). It was underpinned by National Occupational Standards (NOS), the Integrated Competency Framework (ICF) and Core Investigative Doctrine (McGrory and Treacy, 2012; James and Mills, 2012), and it introduced a comprehensive system of training and development, representing what Stelfox (2007) and Kirby (2013) term 'a cradle to grave' structure for the career of an investigator. Aligned to crime seriousness, each level includes the training products available, and indicates the programmes or courses essential for a person to be qualified to investigate at that level. Table 3.1 represents each PIP level, crimes aligned to each level, and the training undertaken in order to qualify. While the alignment to case seriousness is evident, this does not preclude officers dealing with investigations from other levels, usually for pragmatic reasons (James and Mills, 2012).

Training at PIP level one usually takes place as part of the Initial Probationer Learning Development Programme (IPLDP). This is the probationary course police officers receive at the start of their police careers. In order to 'qualify' to undertake PIP level one investigations, officers are required to pass the probationary course and prove competence in the workplace (McGrory and Treacy, 2012). In order to undertake other specific roles within the police organisation at PIP level one, an officer would need to undergo particular training to qualify to perform it. For example, to act as a Specially Trained Officer (STO: a support role for victims of rape or serious sexual assault), officers would be required to undergo specific training in the form of a five-day national training course within a programme of study (STODP). (See Stelfox, 2007, p 40; and McGrory and Treacy, 2012, for further detailed analysis of the individual courses available within PIP).

Table 3.1: Example PIP courses aligned to crime seriousness

Crime seriousness	Example crimes	PIP level	Available courses
Volume crime	Theft, motor vehicle crime, criminal damage	Level one	IPLDP (probationer)* Initial Response Officer (IRO) PEACE interviewing*
Serious and complex Crime	Robbery, rape and other serious sexual offences	Level two	ICIDP (investigator)* ISDP MSCIDP FLO SCAIDP SOIT/STO ABE specialist
Major crime	Murder, manslaughter, stranger rape, kidnap, terrorist offences	Level three	SIO Development Programme*
Major crime	Cross-border and linked series major crimes	Level four	Officer in Overall Command*

*Mandatory in order to be qualified at that level

PIP level two contains the broadest number of investigative programmes. This outlines requirements to qualify as a generalist detective, but it also provides programmes of study for Detective Sergeants (ISDP) and Inspectors (MSCIDP). Additionally, there is a raft of other programmes designed for the specialist investigator. As an example, there are programmes for child abuse investigators (SCAIDP), as well as courses for individuals wishing to perform the role of Family Liaison Officer (FLO) in major crime investigations. In order to undertake any of the roles, officers must fulfil the specialist requirements at PIP level two. Officers wishing to qualify at a higher level of PIP are drawn from the pool of officers at the lower level. Direct entry detectives in the MPS will still be accredited at PIP level one before being eligible for PIP level two training (MPS, 2017).

In order to qualify to deal with serious and complex crime, an officer would need to undertake the Initial Crime Investigator Development Programme (ICIDP). The programme usually takes around 12 months to complete and contains three distinct phases. Phase one is the knowledge acquisition phase. Here, the officer undertakes 14 weeks of self-directed learning according to a specific syllabus including sexual offences, property crime, assaults, drugs, gun crime and evidence (CoP, 2017b). Blackstone's produce the relevant material in *Blackstone's Police Investigators' Manual and Workbook*, updated and published annually (Connor et al, 2016). Following study, students sit an unseen National Investigator Examination (NIE) at phase two, consisting of multiple choice questions aimed at testing students' knowledge, understanding and application of the material (CoP, 2017b). Students must pass the examination in order to enter phase three of the programme (pass mark: 55.7%). The third phase is the skills development phase, designed to equip students with skills to undertake serious and complex investigations. This particular phase is not assessed; officers return to the workplace in order to complete a portfolio of evidence to prove competence. All officers are allocated mentors who are themselves qualified detectives. Their role is to assist in portfolio completion and to advise on practical investigations. Once all phases are complete, investigators qualify as detectives (McGrory and Treacy, 2012). In order to become an SIO, an investigator would usually be required to have completed PIP levels one and two, as well as being at the requisite rank to be an SIO. At present, this could be at DI, DCI or Detective Superintendent (DSupt), depending on the seriousness of the particular investigation. Qualified SIOs are registered with CoP, and are expected to undergo continuous professional development (CPD) (McGrory and Treacy, 2012).

What is striking about many aspects of detective work in the UK is the lack of research into significant aspects of it, including training (Tong, 2005; Brodeur, 2010; James and Mills, 2012). We have seen how much of the research is dated. Major change vehicles such as the PIP programme have a paucity of research too (James and Mills, 2012). The process of PIP has been outlined above, and, in principle, it appears to encompass every aspect of investigator development in a well-structured fashion. It creates development programmes and training courses commensurate with the level of crime seriousness. Alongside the creation of the code of ethics for police officers, and a police college to ensure standards of practice, PIP has been viewed as a beacon of good practice (Flanagan, 2008; Fahsing and Ask, 2016). Indeed, its framework has been lauded by ACPO as an exemplar to be utilised for overall professionalisation of the service (James and Mills, 2012).

Indirect support for PIP comes from research comparing SIOs from the UK with those from Norway. Fahsing and Ask (2016) conducted research with SIOs from both Norway and the UK. They found that UK detectives outperformed their Norwegian counterparts, and, more worryingly, experienced Norwegian detectives were outperformed by students. The researchers attributed such differences to the PIP process in the UK. No similar structure of investigative development exists in Norway and the authors suggested that their findings demonstrate the need for change in investigator development there.

The PIP process has undergone internal review on at least three occasions: in 2008, 2011 and 2013 (CoP, 2014b). As a result, some issues with the process have been highlighted and recommendations for improvement made. One of the most striking revelations was the poor state of continuing professional development (CPD). The PIP process came to the fore amid a fanfare promising professionalisation. Investigators were expected to qualify to perform at the appropriate level, and would then need to comply with CPD requirements in order to maintain qualification. The process was designed to mirror established professions, such as the legal and medical professions, where CPD was embedded. The most recent internal review of PIP (CoP, 2014b) recommended that CoP urgently review the process of CPD to ensure that it met requirements of qualification, registration and continuing development. Historically, officers could qualify for their role and continue to practise for many years without any compulsion to undergo further training. Such a process ignored the fact that knowledge and skills might fade or become outdated over time. Efforts to embed CPD within PIP have thus far been few (it is a part of PIP level three), although a process is now emerging (CoP, 2016b).

In order to ensure consistency in relation to professional development, recommendations were made to establish a PIP accreditation register where those qualified would be easily identifiable. The report noted that Home Office statistics on Police Service Strength in EW) did not distinguish the numbers of qualified PIP detectives, nor was it able to quantify detectives in relation to rank, race or gender (Home Office, 2011). It estimated that there were around 29,000 detectives in EW (CoP, 2014b). The report went on to recommend officers complete a PIP learning portfolio, charting their progress and readily accessible when they wish to apply for advancement. It remains to be seen whether these proposed developments will indeed produce supportive mechanisms for practitioners, or whether they reflect the rhetoric rather than reality of professional development of investigators In 2005, Centrex announced an intention to write a CPD process for investigators. Almost a decade later, the most recent PIP review called for this to be considered as a matter of urgency (CoP, 2014b). It is regrettable that such a crucial part of professionalisation remained neglected for so long. Recently, CoP published a CPD document (CoP, 2016b) outlining the future CPD framework within the service. CoP posit the use of CPD as a means to both maintain and enhance professional capacity, and they frame the process as part of a commitment to lifelong learning. The overall responsibility rests with the individual officer, although there is a distinction made between individual, role, and local and national CPD requirements. CoP will eventually provide CPD requirements for all roles, although this is still at an early stage of development. The process appears flexible in relation to what constitutes CPD, and specifically suggests that attendance at a training event would only constitute CPD if reflected on in relation to practice. Officers are provided with a CPD toolkit to assist them in deciding on their individual requirements (CoP, 2016c). While these developments are welcome, independent research should be undertaken to assess its utility. Will it become yet another tick-box exercise that does little to develop or maintain professional practice?

A recent House of Commons Home Affairs Committee (2016) suggested that CoP lacked internal recognition and respect from practitioners. Examples of this related to the failure of forces to embrace the new code of ethics, designed as a pivotal factor in the professionalisation movement. A further HMIC report, highlighted inconsistencies in the training of new recruits and recommended central training or regional hubs to try to improve this issue. These recommendations reassert the importance of consistent training across the country. Evidently, the present system does not allow that to happen because of regional variations (HMIC, 2016). At a time when consideration is being given to the idea of higher education involvement in police training, consistency is an important issue. A number of important questions arise. Is consistency to be achieved if there are a diverse number of higher education institutions offering degrees? Will that be achieved by CoP setting out core requirements for higher education programmes? Will the police want a significant amount of police training content to appear within undergraduate degrees? Commentators have identified the differences between training and education (Hallenberg, 2012), so it will be interesting to see how these new arrangements take shape, particularly when there is a large amount of income to be earned by higher education institutions in the policing sphere. It must also be reiterated that CoP has struggled to manage consistency across 43 forces. How will consistency *improve* if there is a proliferation of the training to higher education Institutions?

James and Mills (2012) conducted a small-scale research study on the implementation of PIP, driven by an ACPO suggestion that the PIP framework should be seen as an exemplar in relation to the professionalisation of policing as a whole. The study interviewed senior officers and detectives in one force area. The researchers recognised the limitations of their study and encouraged further research on PIP. Describing their research as a case study (in the context of PIP in one police force), semi-structured interviews were conducted with senior officers, while questionnaires were utilised with detectives. It is suspected that the reason for the different methodologies was because the interviews were likely to be with a smaller number of officers than the potential respondents for the questionnaire. In any event, the Chief Constable and Deputy Chief Constable were among the senior officer cohort, and ten officers responded to the questionnaire. James and Mills (2012) found recurring themes militated against PIP, such as 'organisational culture'. They describe a female officer who felt that investigative ability was secondary to consideration of whether a person's face fitted. Whether this is police culture or a specific detective culture at play is an interesting point. Detective culture has been said to consist of increased scepticism, extra secrecy and camaraderie, and chauvinistic and conservative attitudes (Skolnick, 1966; Punch, 1983; Hobbs, 1988; Maguire and Norris, 1992, 1994). Whether this still pervades detective work in the same way today is open to conjecture, but James and Mills appear to find traces of it in this small study.

Other issues highlighted were the effects of a target-driven culture and under-resourcing on the investigative effectiveness of officers. Officers were required to do more with less resource, and there appeared to be a disparity between the level of crimes a PIP level two detective was trained to investigate and an expectation from senior officers that they could also investigate volume crimes. Sometimes, this appeared to be due to lack of faith in the uniformed officer's competency levels. While the decision to allocate volume crimes to a detective might be reasonable, they are trained to deal with more serious crime. Whenever they deal with volume crimes, they are prevented from dealing with more serious crime, an issue raised in a report on crime management (Audit Commission, 1993, p 1). The theory for some time was that the CID would be utilised to deal with more serious crime because of their perceived greater specialism, although this was not managed well (Maguire and Norris, 1992). Chatterton (2008) noted how the under-resourcing of GOCID was having a detrimental effect on performance, morale and stress. He also found that there was little management buy-in to the principles of PIP, with commitment to professional practice often subservient to organisational outcome measures. This present study suggests there are further frustrations with the organisation of detective work. James and Mills (2012) also highlight the falling numbers of staff applying to be detectives owing to (among other things) better shift arrangements for uniformed officers and a less stressful professional life. At present, the PIP process demands much of a student to qualify, yet the rewards for doing so are symbolic rather than economic. Police officers are not paid for their level of specialism but are remunerated through the rigid national pay scales. A recent HMIC report (HMIC, 2017) confirms a shortage of detectives nationally, with forces now planning direct entry detectives (MPS, 2017) or streamlining officers for detective posts (Thames Valley, Hampshire and Norfolk).

The issue of the perceived ability of the uniformed branch to deal effectively and efficiently with volume crime investigations is a cause for concern, particularly as it has been raised in the past. In this present study it was raised by a senior police officer. The Audit Commission (1993) found evidence of poor competence in relation to uniform investigation of crime. They suggested a number of reasons for this, including a pervading attitude that crime was a detective function, poor supervision, that officers lacked time to be able to conduct investigations properly, and notably that there was a lack of training. While there have been efforts to remedy this in relation to the changing face of probationary training, and now PIP level one training, it is a real concern to see senior officers suggesting that there is a lack of competence in PIP level one investigators. If this was to be reflected nationally, one would need to ask serious questions about the effectiveness of PIP.

Current content

At PIP level two (ICIDP), recent years have seen a gradual decline in the number of weeks at the skills development stage. This phase has variously been 14 weeks (1987), ten weeks (prior to PIP), eight weeks (prior to PIP), and six weeks plus interview training. It now encompasses just four weeks' training. Of those four weeks, one week includes general investigative inputs around areas such as crime scene management, and principles of investigation. One week is dedicated to public protection, and one week is dedicated to the use of technology in investigations. The final week allows for a Hydra-related exercise (an immersive-learning decision-making exercise) and one day of local, tailored materials. Barely half a day is dedicated specifically to decision-making, although evidently this is threaded throughout the training (CoP, 2014b). Because of the absence of research in this area, it is difficult to discern where skill development occurs, although this may not be evident until the investigator provides evidence of competence for their portfolio (CoP, 2014b). While numbers of training weeks is not indicative of any drop in standards, proponents of the PIP regime would point to the fact that law and policy are now dealt with adequately by phase one of the programme (McGrory and Treacy, 2012). They would also argue that modern investigators are constantly required to keep up to date with essential e-learning, accessible via NCALT, and that they have access to the PNLD and APP at their fingertips. On the other hand, it could be asserted that a paucity of time spent on decision-making, MOJ, IPCC cases, and even CPIA is suggestive at worst of an ignorance of crucial issues, or at best an exercise in risk management. HMIC (2014a) recently noted the scaling-back of training departments and cuts to training budgets, urging forces to consider staff development within financial constraints. This may create an over-reliance on technological advances to the detriment of real development.

E-learning

There is little research on the effectiveness of e-learning within the police (Benson and Powell, 2015), although what does exist appears positive (Donovant, 2009; Benson and Powell, 2015). It has its benefits in terms of cost efficiency (weighed against face to face training time and abstractions), flexibility and accessibility, and staff development (Benson and Powell, 2015). Despite these positive perspectives, e-learning has received criticism in relation to DA training (HMIC, 2014b). While e-learning can bring a multitude of technological innovations to aid learning, such as avatars, and sequential learning programmes, the description of their use within the police service relates to a more narrow approach (i.e. online material to be viewed in a short time-frame, followed by a basic exam or quiz). HMIC (2004) describe it as typically where material is read on-screen, followed by multiple-choice questions to test knowledge and understanding. The proliferation of this type of learning within the police can be viewed as an attempt to embrace new and developing technology and as a pragmatic response to austerity. However, utilised in the manner described, it could fail to attain the depth of knowledge and understanding required, particularly in high-risk areas of policing. The HMIC state: 'HMIC sees little, if any, value in e-learning as an effective training method as it limits the opportunity for discussion, reflection and checking understanding' (HMIC, 2014b, p 9).

The HMIC went on to describe how certain forces supplemented e-learning with face-to-face contact at briefings. This can evidently be undertaken effectively at little extra cost, although this is doubtful, particularly within a briefing environment where operational matters tend to take precedence. The potential for inconsistency in delivery is of concern.

Honess (2016) conducted research into police officer perceptions of NCALT. He found that officers often failed to see the value of e-learning, being sceptical of the system and seeing it primarily as a tick-box exercise for disciplinary purposes. As Honess observes, e-learning has its place, utilised effectively, but if executed poorly, with a poor reputation among grassroots practitioners, it is unlikely (on its own) to be the answer to cost-effective training and education, assuming that such training is the only means of enhancing professional knowledge and education.

Chapters 2 and 3 have discussed the development of investigative practice and training in light of a perceived move away from art and craft towards a more scientific research-based approach. There is much research that can be undertaken to populate both of these important areas. However, a recent CoP pronouncement appears to herald a subtle shift back to the dominance of craft in investigations. In 2013, CoP announced that it would be moving away from attendance on courses, with greater concentration on e-learning, peer learning, operational experience, and workplace observations. Justification for the move was the costly nature of training and development of officers, as well as the time spent on courses. Does this represent an organisation wedded to professionalisation? Or does it say something about the depth of cuts and attempts to deal with them?

Conclusion

This chapter has attempted to trace the development of detective training from its early years to the present day. Some themes emerge that demonstrate a willingness to embrace professionalisation, although latest pronouncements appear to suggest otherwise. Some detective training has undergone significant change in the last few decades, particularly in relation to investigative interviewing. This area has appeared to benefit the most from evidence-based practice by harnessing research in the field of psychology to significantly improve both the training and practice of interviewing suspects, victims and witnesses, although it is clear there is no room for complacency. Theory and research suggests that the move from searching for a confession to finding the truth is here, that officers no longer hold the confession to be the most important evidence, and that there is a thorough search for evidence and a recording and disclosure of it even if it potentially exonerates a suspect (Runciman, 1993). Whether this is the reality of modern investigations is open to debate and appears to be another fertile area for potential research. On paper, the PIP process is a clear developmental pathway for investigators, and a framework through which training effort can be focused. The more serious the crime, the more training a person requires in order to be able to qualify to investigate it. So far, so good. Each programme of study is known, the content is designed to ensure national minimum standards, so in theory any qualified officer should be able to deal with the investigation of crime (at their PIP level) in any part of the country. This brings with it a good degree of consistency across the UK. Programmes no longer concentrate the majority of their time on teaching law. There are often distinct phases of pre-learning, skills acquisition and skill development in the workplace, so that the investigator has a chance to develop and apply their learning in the workplace. On the face of it, everything appears to be worlds away from the development of detectives in the past. Yet much of the practice is under-researched, including the skills and abilities required to be effective as an investigator in the modern era. The following chapter will consider the issue of investigative decision-making, and efforts made to ensure that this too reflects the modern professionalisation agenda.

Further reading

James, A. and Mills, M. (2012) 'Does ACPO know best: to what extent may the PIP programme provide a template for the professionalization of policing?' *The Police Journal*, 85: 133–49.

McGrory, D. and Treacy, P. (2012) The Professionalising Investigation Programme. In Haberfield, M.R., Clarke, C.A., and Sheridan, D.L. (eds) *Police organisation and training*. London: Springer, pp 113–36.

Stelfox, P. (2009) *Criminal investigation: An introduction to principles and practice*. Cullompton: Willan Publishing.

FOUR

Decision-making

Introduction

Poor decision-making is often said to be linked to wrongful convictions and other MOJs. In research for the RCCJ, Maguire and Norris (1992) identified decision-making as one of the most common reasons for MOJs. They suggested that detective training should include this issue in a more fundamental way. Decision-making skills have been highlighted as crucial to detective practice (Smith and Flanagan, 2000; O'Neill, 2011; Westera et al, 2014). Some attempts have been made to address decision making in the form of guidance in homicide investigations (ACPO, 2006) and general investigations (ACPO, Centrex, 2005). CD posits an open-minded, methodical approach, calling on investigators to use a sceptical and inquiring mindset, accepting nothing at face value. Investigative interview practice was significantly altered to ensure information seeking rather than confessions (Bull, 2014). Since 2012, officers have utilised a decision-making model to assist them. Yet cases continue to fail due to poor decision-making (see Chapter 7). Why do failures recur? Is it a cultural issue? Is it systemic? Or, is it due to human fallibility? This chapter begins with discussion of relevant research that considers attempts to explain errors in decision-making. The chapter then critically analyses modern investigative practice and models of investigation. Has research in this area influenced police practice in the same way as psychological research did in the development of investigative interviewing? Fahsing (2016) argues that much decision-making research is descriptive and fails to identify what works for the benefit of practitioners.

A snapshot of relevant research

Decision-making, problem-solving, reasoning and critical thinking are all distinct areas in the academic literature, and each has its own set of theoretical perspectives and a large body of supporting literature. There is, however, a distinct overlap between some of the perspectives. Judgement and decision-making is an area that has produced many different theoretical perspectives. For instance, naturalistic decision-making (NDM) concerns decision-making in complex and demanding situations. Much work has been undertaken in the military context, as well as in policing (such as critical incident management) to try to discover what cognitive processes are utilised by individuals in such high-pressure situations. Another perspective, closely linked to NDM and perhaps responsible for its rise in the academic literature, is explanation-based decision-making (EBDM). A seminal paper on EBDM by Hastie and Pennington (2000) discusses how EBDM attempts to describe how people make important decisions in a range of formal and informal settings. Studies have shown that, as a prelude to making important decisions, people evaluate pieces of evidence before deciding on an appropriate course of action (Hastie and Pennington, 1986, 1995). Hastie and Pennington (2000), describe how jurors tend to listen to the evidence and then construct a mental model (described as a story) from what they have heard. Their mental model represents an explanation of the evidence. Hastie and Pennington (2000), suggest that individuals then make decisions based on the mental model they have constructed, not based on the evidence as was originally received. At the same time, the individual also creates alternatives from which to choose an appropriate course of action.

While this research was conducted in the field of jury decision-making, there is much to suggest that this is how *all* humans make decisions. What EBDM posits is that the decision should not be the main focus of research. What is most important is what goes on in the construction of the mental models prior to the decision. Jones (2000), conducted a study of the decision-making process of investigators involved in a simulated serious crime investigation. He described an investigative decision-making cycle that began with information, moved to interpretation, then to an investigative decision that determined investigative direction. Though in different contexts, what both of the above studies demonstrate is that much of what occurs in decision-making processes begins with interpretation of incoming information. In the juror study, evidence is placed into a mental model. At this point inferences are being drawn, and evaluations and judgements are being made about evidential reliability and quality. Cognitive filters are being applied to sort good evidence from the bad in order to inform the mental model. Similarly, investigators interpret evidence at a point before making decisions and setting goals and directions of the investigation. In fact, assuming rationality, it is arguable that some form of evaluation and making sense of available cues will have preceded *every* decision. The investigative task is no different at the volume crime level. Investigators must assess the value of information when it comes into an investigation and make sense of where and how it fits with other information and evidence. At all stages of a criminal investigation, at whatever level, investigators will be drawing inferences from material, and engaging in different forms of reasoning (Carson, 2009b). They need to be alert to dangers of drawing conclusions based on faulty logic, and be alert to making assumptions (Fahsing and Gottschalk, 2008).

Hammond et al (1998) discussed decision-making traps. They warned that several human failings can hinder good decision-making. They suggest: 'The way our human brain works can sabotage our decisions' (Hammond et al, 1998, p 47).

Moreover, humans utilise a complex set of unconscious routines when engaging in decision-making. Called heuristics, these routines are usually accurate. However, there are situations in which they will be assumed to be accurate when in fact they are not. These situations can lead to detrimental consequences. Heuristics can be characterised as irrational thoughts, biases or misinterpretations. What Hammond et al (1998) depict are deeply ingrained thought processes that are often invisible and consequently impossible to recognise. Kassin et al (2003) suggests that once people form impressions, they do everything they can to find evidence to support their prevailing theory. Nickerson (1998) describes this type of phenomenon as confirmatory bias (CB) (see also Burke, 2006). That is: 'The seeking or interpreting of evidence in ways that are partial to existing beliefs or a hypothesis in hand' (Nickerson, 1998, p 175).

According to Evans (1989), CB is one of the most pervasive forms of reasoning identified by psychological literature. Police investigators are humans too and will thus be prone to the same errors. Worryingly, Nickerson (1998) suggests that because CB is prevalent in human cognition, often it is undertaken unwittingly. He distinguishes between motivated and unmotivated CB. The former relates to where an individual is motivated to defend existing beliefs, whereas the other connotes a more unconscious process. In either case, Nickerson points out that once a position is taken by an individual, any subsequent search for evidence is for confirmation of that position, not disconfirmation. The decision-maker is also prone to attempt to justify their position. Nickerson (1998) suggested CB manifests itself in the following ways.

First, there is a tendency to restrict oneself to the favoured position. Conflicting possibilities or beliefs are ignored and supportive evidence preferred. Disconfirmatory evidence is given too little weight, whereas confirmatory evidence is given exaggerated weight. In short, the process will be to confirm initial diagnosis rather than to objectively search for the truth (Maguire and Norris, 1992). Accordingly, if a person looks hard enough, they will be able to find what they want to find. This kind of thinking resonates with the idea of case construction posited by McConville et al (1991), who suggest that detectives often form a view of guilt and construct a case based on that perception, ignoring evidence that might disconfirm and exonerate. In effect, a conclusion reached in this way is adopted and maintained (Burke, 2006; Findley and Scott, 2006; Fraser-McKenzie and Dror 2009).

Such thinking concurs with the work of Fahsing and Ask (2013), who conducted an interview study with 35 homicide detectives from the UK and Norway (20 from the UK, 15 from Norway). The detectives worked in four different areas in each country, and a small number had retired before the study began. Experienced detectives were asked to detail what they felt were the most important factors that led an investigation from a suspect *identification* stage to a suspect *verification* stage. In effect, the verification stage assumes that the investigation has the right suspect and the material is then marshalled towards a court outcome. This is the stage of investigation that is arguably most under-researched (Brodeur, 2010). Respondents cited the decision to name, arrest or charge a suspect as a tipping point, as well as when particular strategies, hypotheses or courses of action were chosen. The authors suggested that further research should be undertaken to consider the effect that tipping points have on performance of tasks. This is a very interesting area that does indeed appear ripe for further research. If an investigation appears to have moved from suspect identification towards verification, then what does that mean for lines of inquiry deemed merely superfluous to the prevailing case theory? Take the example of Colin Stagg. When officers were convinced that Stagg was the man who killed Rachel Nickel, other potential suspects and information about their activities appeared to remain in the system (including that of Robert Napper, eventually convicted of the killing [Cerfontyne, 2010]). This same process also occurred in other high-profile cases, such as the Maxwell Confait murder investigation in the early 1970s. In that case, all other lines of inquiry were effectively closed once three suspects were assumed guilty. A tipping point is the point where an investigation is considered in the light of all of the information and evidence available and a decision is made to seek a charging decision from CPS. This is a necessary process within any investigation. The problem arises when the tipping point comes *too early*, meaning that the focus on one particular suspect dominates all subsequent enquiries to the extent that other information and disconfirmatory evidence is ignored (Rossomo, 2008). There are circumstances too where a tipping point is reached not around the identity of a suspect but around suspect attributes. This too becomes problematic if the initial decision as to why those are the suspect's attributes is flawed. This occurred most famously in the Yorkshire Ripper investigation, when investigators relied on a tape from Wearside Jack as being the voice of the killer. All subsequent strategies were geared to eliminating individuals as suspects who did not have a Wearside accent. Unfortunately, Peter Sutcliffe was eliminated as a very good suspect because he came from Bradford (see Brookman, 2005 for details of the media call for knowledge of the author of the letter and tape).

Rassin (2010), conducted a study of police officers (58), judges (44), and prosecutors (16). Using a vignette involving a homicide, two versions of the vignette were distributed to participants, one with a suspect, Eva, the other with suspect Eva but also with sufficient information to provide an alternative suspect. Rassin (2010) found that police, prosecutors and judges asked to rate whether Eva was innocent or guilty on a 100-point scale were blind to alternatives once a strong suspect became evident. This study supported earlier research, which found that police officers were blind to alternatives when they had a personal need for closure (Ask and Granhag, 2005). Studies therefore seem to suggest that CB is a potential problem within investigations, and one hypothesis is formed while credible alternatives are ignored.

McConville et al (1991) suggest that detectives have not traditionally sought the truth. Often they become convinced of a suspect's guilt, and with that mindset seek evidence to confirm guilt. This position is supported by research, which found that 70% of investigative practitioners were convinced of guilt prior to interview (Stephenson and Moston, 1994). Such a perspective gives scant regard to alternative possibilities. Brodeur (2010) noted that Canadian detectives routinely broke rules to ensure that those they considered guilty were convicted and given their just deserts. Such practices have seemingly been condoned by the rest of the criminal justice system too, in order to ensure that the 'right' people are convicted, even if the means to secure convictions were dubious (Chatterton, 2008). Unfortunately, the problem comes when judgement of guilt is flawed (the case of R v Kiszko is a good example). This type of thinking also underlies the ends/means justification of the Dirty Harry problem, where a firm belief in the guilt of a suspect underlies dirty means employed to ensure a (so-called) morally justifiable outcome (Klockars, 1980). What cognitive processes (conscious or unconscious) place investigators into this position are unclear. Sometimes they may be deliberate thoughts, feelings and motivations, while on other occasions they may be less conscious. CB is also similar to tunnel vision. A good example of tunnel vision occurred in a case in the Netherlands in 2000 (van Koppen, 2008). A man was convicted of the sexual assault and murder of a young child, and the sexual assault of the child's friend in a park in the Netherlands. The striking feature of the case was the fact that the surviving child ran from the park following the attack and waved down a passing cyclist. The authorities were notified and the police began to conduct an investigation. Suspicion fell on the passing cyclist, who investigations uncovered had previously been warned in the park for approaching young children in suspicious circumstances. Police investigators were convinced that the suspect was the perpetrator, despite the surviving child providing a description unlike him and not identifying him as the perpetrator. In addition, police found DNA. This did not match the man on the cycle. This case provides a striking example of tunnel vision. Police (and subsequently prosecutors) were so convinced of the suspect's guilt that they explained all of the pieces of evidence that pointed away from the cyclist as offender. The child's descriptions and lack of identification were explained away as trauma, and the DNA evidence was suggestive of an accomplice, not the fact that the cyclist was innocent. Years later, DNA was matched to a known criminal who was convicted of the murder and sexual assaults. The cyclist was indeed innocent (van Koppen, 2008). It is exactly this kind of case that illustrates the problems of tunnel vision, CB and belief persistence. A subsequent public inquiry in the Netherlands recommended ways to eliminate tunnel vision within major crime investigations, including a 'contrarian' role undertaken by other senior detectives during each investigation. The role attempted to ensure that investigations did not fall into the trap of tunnel vision, with little success (Salet and Terpstra, 2014).

Research has also highlighted issues such as the primacy effect (Nickerson, 1998). Belief persistence connotes circumstances where early impressions are formed and people maintain them despite the presence of clear, contradictory evidence (Rossomo, 2008; Fraser-McKenzie and Dror, 2009). Rossomo (2008) also considered how heuristics and biases can contribute to MOJs. Wrongful convictions may be thankfully rare nowadays, although it is doubtful whether any meaningful research could be conducted to determine whether this is the case or not, or whether attempts to minimise them have succeeded. Research is unlikely to be able to uncover a true picture because, by their very nature, they tend to surface many years after they have occurred. Yet there is now a wider sense in which MOJs occur. Wrongful convictions are but one facet of MOJs, and encompass cases where the guilty party has been exonerated for a crime (and thus not been imprisoned for their misdemeanours), and where police conduct such poor investigations that no person is brought to justice; for example, where genuine victims are denied access to the criminal justice system and their complaints go uninvestigated (Savage and Milne, 2007; Poyser and Milne, 2015).

The latter examples appear to be more prevalent in cases such as rape, domestic abuse, missing persons or where a victim has mental health issues (see Chapter 7 in relation to IPCC investigations). In each of these cases, one could argue that, consciously or unconsciously, there appear to be biases, judgements, myth acceptance or judgemental attitudes that ensure that these types of cases are given insufficient attention. Just as important as the wrongful conviction cases, numerous cases are emerging where victims are denied access to the criminal justice system or receive a poor service from the investigative arm of the criminal justice system. As Cook and Tattersall (2014) attest, this can include examples where officers have previously dealt with false allegations of rape, and this subsequently colours their responses to further reports. The investigator may assume that the later reports are also untrue, and this will determine the amount of effort expended to investigate thoroughly or provide justification for a higher amount of effort expended to disprove a report (Cook and Tattersall, 2014, pp 27–8). Denying access to the criminal justice system or judging a report or victim to be unworthy of investigative effort will not necessarily be a conscious decision made by practitioners, for the reasons described by Hammond and Nickerson, above. Even when investigative decisions are made that reflect these heuristics and biases, often they are not likely to be visible or open to scrutiny unless the victim complains or they become cases where obvious gross failures are present (Goldstein, 1960, p 552). As Goldstein (1960) notes, decisions *not* to invoke the criminal law or the criminal process are incapable of effective control. One of the key elements in modern-day investigations designed to control such decisions is accountability through decision-making. There has for many years been an expectation that police investigators write down their decisions (CoP, 2017a).

On a final note, Lepard and Campbell (2009) suggest that many wrongful convictions occur in cases where a systematic approach to investigations is absent. They argue that police organisations require a strong commitment to ethical standards, allied to a systematic approach to investigations, and that in order for this approach to become embedded, officers should receive regular training on the known or suspected causes of wrongful convictions. We have seen in the preceding chapters how this is unlikely to occur at present given time constraints on detective training. In addition, prevailing guidance lacks a systematic thinking model for investigation. In the following section, police practice in the form of investigative models will be discussed, together with a discussion around modern expectations of record-keeping.

The practice

The history of decision-making within criminal investigations is littered with high-profile failures and MOJs. These can provide a distorted view of the system and how it works. From a naïve point of view, it is arguable that the majority of cases are completed without problem. Cases are either filed with no further investigation possible, or they proceed through the criminal justice system seamlessly. Seen in this light, high-profile failures and MOJ cases are exceptional aberrations in an otherwise healthy system. On the other hand, one could argue, cases that come to light reveal a more endemic problem. On this view, we only hear about the tip of the iceberg. MOJs go unnoticed unless somehow brought to the Appeal Courts or public attention. Whether problems are systemic or part of human nature is open to question. Decisions within criminal investigations start at the gate of the criminal justice system. One of the first decisions is whether the person reporting a crime is worthy of the term 'victim' and whether their report amounts to a criminal offence. There have been several cases (mainly in relation to reports of rape, serious sexual offences, or domestic abuse) where victims have been denied access to the system.

In EW, attempts to produce guidance for investigators have been few, with reliance placed on either experience, academic textbooks (most notably Hans Gross, 1906), materials produced by police leaders (Vincent, 1888, cited in Moore and Rubin, 2014), or retired police officers (Morrish, 1940; see Chapter 1 for further discussion). These publications contained little regarding the *process* of decision-making within criminal investigations. The first official attempts to provide a guide for modern investigators was the *Murder Investigation Manual* (MIM), conceived and produced due to the anticipated loss of skills and experience with SIO retirements in the late 1990s, and as a reaction to failings in the Stephen Lawrence investigation (Macpherson, 1999; Brookman, 2005).

The MIM has been credited with providing a useful starting point for investigators. The Home Office has since suggested that major crime investigation should be seen as an exemplar for all investigations

(Home Office, 2001a). ACPO credits MIM with heralding a response to homicide investigation based on scientific principles (Tong et al, 2009). Is this the case? What the MIM does is define a set of tactics and strategies that can be employed in any major crime investigation. Providing also a set of stages to an investigation in the form of a process map, the MIM contains several chapters describing strategies and actions that an SIO could choose to utilise (Brookman, 2005; Tong et al, 2009; Stelfox, 2009; Cook and Tattersall, 2014). Prior to the MIM, there was a cyclical process in relation to how SIOs learnt. They may very well have been experienced detectives, and they may have investigated major crimes under the tutelage of an experienced SIO (but not always, the police organisation having a rank orientation that assumes ability and competence in a particular role, the higher the rank of the individual). Whatever the experience of the officer, they would still be learning the SIO role as soon as they began to perform it. Much of their learning was through experience and practice. Little was written down to assist them. They would make their mistakes, learn from them, become experienced as SIOs and then move on or retire. New SIOs would then arrive, and they too would repeat the cycle. The MIM represented the capturing of collective SIO experience, to allow new and seasoned practitioners alike to be able to consult one resource for assistance. Rather like a library, the MIM provides a number of strategies and tactics that can be taken from the shelf to be employed, and it is for the SIO to decide which to employ in an investigation. As a crude example, if someone is murdered in a public place and the police seek witnesses and suspects, a good communications strategy (including a media appeal), might be a worthwhile pursuit (among other strategies). On the other hand, if a suspect is caught leaving a shop with a number of goods that have not been paid for, then a media appeal might be of limited value. Rather, the lead investigator in the latter case might employ strategies to gain witness accounts, CCTV evidence, and interview the suspect. For a major crime, an SIO would be expected to record decisions in a policy file. In order to assist SIO decision-making, the MIM contains what is described as a model of the 'idealised decision making process' (IM). This is credited to Oldfield (1998), although the reference in the MIM is absent.

Following report of a potentially serious crime, the IM suggests that investigators ask a series of questions. These are staged from the beginning of the event in question, and include questions such as: 'What immediate uniformed response is required?; What immediate detective response is required?; What does the investigation now know?; What does this tell you about what might have happened?' (ACPO, 2006, p 55).

Following the perceived success of the MIM and with a renewed crime-fighting agenda from the government of the day, the issue of investigative skills and the need for an investigative doctrine loomed large. The National Centre for Policing Excellence (NCPE) was created as a result of the Police Reform Act 2002, and tasked with creating an investigative doctrine for modern policing. Core Investigative Doctrine (CD) was intended to be a constituent part of 'doctrine'. In evidence to a House of Commons Committee in 2004, members of NCPE suggested that doctrine encompassed:

- codified statutory endorsement;
- guidance ratified by the Home Office (and part of HMIC inspections);
- practice advice not mandated.

CD represented the last of these, designed to provide evidence of investigative good practice (Select Committee on Home Affairs, 2005).

CD was described in its opening pages as 'a strategic overview of the investigative process, providing a framework for investigative good practice. Its purpose is to provide investigators with the skills and knowledge they require to conduct investigations in a competent manner, inspiring confidence in the investigator and the wider criminal justice system' (ACPO, Centrex, 2005, p 1) Interestingly, it was meant to act as a starting point for further research to ensure that it was evidence-based and current (ACPO, Centrex, 2005, p 16). There is a paucity of research on the MIM or CD or any aspects of it. Additionally, whether a document is able to provide 'skills' is open to debate. That said, CD was intended to complement the PIP process. We have seen in the previous chapter that the skills development phase is both the course and experiential development, proven by workplace competencies, and compliance with CD.

CD comprised two distinct parts. Part One contained aspects of the knowledge required to perform the role of investigator, particularly in relation to key areas of legislation such as PACE, CPIA, HRA and RIPA. The overarching tenet of this part is that an investigator cannot properly perform their role if they do not have a working knowledge of legislation. Part Two provided a process map of a criminal investigation. It then provided very detailed and specific advice and guidance in relation to each of the areas of the process (including strategies and actions that could be employed). The process map provides a series of stages that might occur if an investigation was to begin with a report through to a conclusion at court, accepting that some investigations will conclude or begin at different points and that they may be resolved by disposals other than a charge or summons. The stages of the process are identified in Figure 4.1. CD attempted to provide some recognisable points within an investigation where decision-making was applied in a reflective manner. The police had been accused in the past of failing to think through their investigations (Laycock, 2003). According to CD, once an initial investigation into a crime was concluded, this represented a useful time for investigators to consider the position of the investigation. In truth, many cases can be reflected on at this point, assuming that sufficient investigation has been undertaken at the initial

Figure 4.1: Process map of a typical investigation

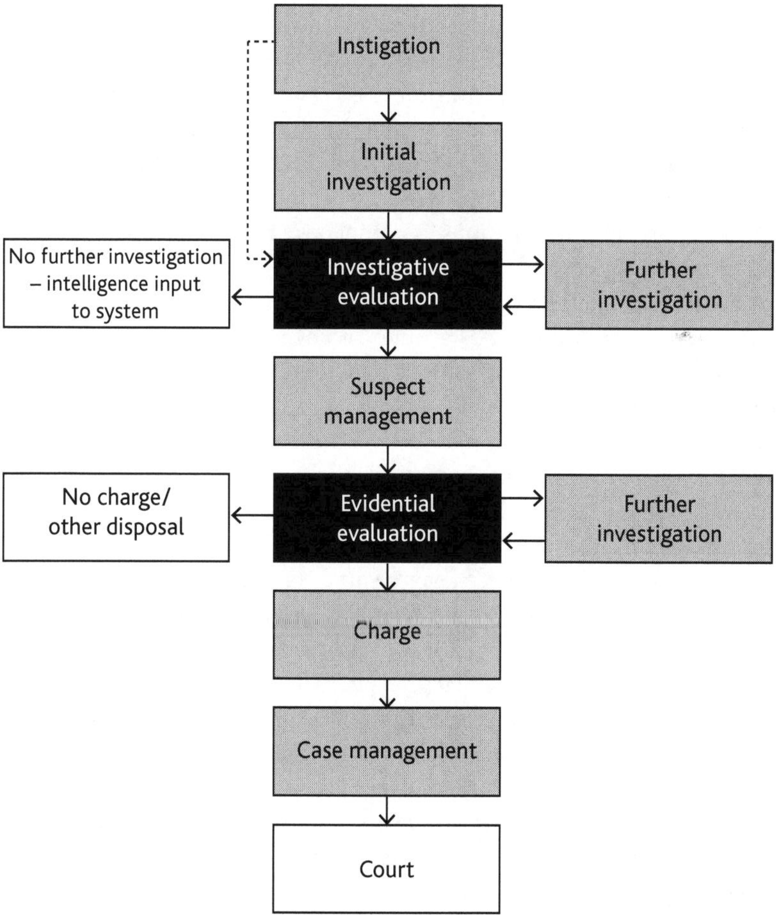

Source: CoP, 2016a.
Note: Gray sections represent activities from investigative strategies, black sections represent the main decision points and the white sections are the outcomes that can be achieved.

investigation stage, and decisions can be made to either file the case (with no further lines of inquiry to pursue), or to decide that the case merits further investigation. Depending on the level of seriousness of a crime, the first evaluation may be undertaken by staff acting for the purposes of screening, or crime management units designed to allocate crimes to investigators that have potential leads.

The initial investigative evaluation, if it highlights further investigation is necessary, may also provide an investigative plan for investigators to pursue (ACPO, 2001). The nominated investigator will be responsible for investigating from that point onwards. Depending on complexity and seriousness of the investigation, the investigator may conduct a number of investigative evaluations until either no suspect is identified (in which case the investigation is filed as undetected) or they identify a suspect, in which case they continue into the suspect management phase of the model. Stelfox (2009) notes the iterative nature of the investigative process, from evaluation to further investigation, back to evaluation (and so on), in order to come to a solution. To aid an investigator, CD posits some principles and a mindset designed to encourage an open-minded professional approach to the endeavour. CD suggests that officers should use the investigative mindset throughout their investigations. It comprises a number of facets, notably described by the acronym UPERE, the ABC of crime, and an approach to the material gathered that is questioning and intent on discovering gaps in what is known (For a fuller discussion of both UPERE and the ABC of crime, see CoP, 2016a and Stelfox, 2009). Together, these encourage officers to analyse all material gathered in a detailed and systematic fashion in order to assess its provenance and reliability against what is already known in the investigation, to apply a gap analysis to identify what else may be sought within the inquiry, and to have a healthy sceptical approach to all incoming information. This approach encourages investigators to never assume that the material gathered is accurate or reliable until it has been analysed and considered against what is already known. This is useful guidance that might go some way towards nullifying any primacy effect, belief persistence, availability error or CB. The investigative mindset is encouraged throughout an investigation, but will be most evident within both the investigative and evidential evaluation stages.

CD provided some useful guidance to investigators. It discussed heuristics and biases, and potential human failings (including CB), albeit not to any great extent (Bryant, 2009a). References to gap analysis and the ABC of crime also encourage thoroughness, while investigative and evidential evaluations urge investigators to conduct reviews at key stages to enable them to gauge the progress of them. If, as envisaged, all investigators utilised this practice, and understood the principles of CD, then investigations would be undertaken consistently, and more thorough investigations would ensue. CD does not, however, encourage the use of hypotheses. While accepting that they may be useful, they condone them only in proscribed circumstances, where all information has been obtained. Couching it in these terms misunderstands the purpose of hypotheses and restricts their use. In fact, the failure to weave hypothesis development into the heart of the decision-making process arguably omits the strategic thread of an investigation that could enable more focused investigations. Hypothesis development would not only encourage consideration of alternative possibilities, but would ensure that an investigator tests hypotheses.

Recently, the idea of proportional justice has become a mantra in criminal justice circles. It celebrates that in sentencing, for instance, those responsible for criminal acts receive their just deserts. In investigative circles, it has come to mean not only that the less serious the crime, the less investigative effort needs to be expended, but also anecdotally that investigators can decide on a disposal outcome first, and then commence a proportional investigation towards that outcome. Such an approach risks taking open-minded objectivity out of an investigation and promotes practice that developments since the turn of the century have attempted to eliminate – that is, making decisions prematurely, before conducting an investigation. The promotion of proportionality is not surprising given financial constraints and scarce resources. What it does is raise the question as to the appropriate model and guidance for volume crime investigations in contrast to serious, complex and major crime. Is it reasonable to expect a scaled-down version of guidance for high volume crime cases, or should the principles of investigation be the same for all crime? What effect would a different model at the lower level have for investigator development at a later stage? There is little research on the effectiveness of CD, whether officers utilise it beyond PIP accreditation, or whether it is utilised by practitioners after training. In addition to the MIM and CD, a National Decision Model (NDM) is now in place, evidently relevant to all decision-making within policing. The following section will consider the model in more detail. O'Neill (2011) asked investigators how they investigated crime: 62.5% were trained PIP investigators (or equivalent). Not one suggested that they used CD or its process model to investigate crime. When asked to elaborate on the process they used (and where they acquired it), many indicated they used their own model, honed by previous practice, not training.

The National Decision Model

The 2008 Flanagan review of policing appears to have been a catalyst for the development of the NDM. Suggesting that police resources were facing increasing demands that were exacerbated by too much bureaucracy, Flanagan advocated a more proportionate response based on threat risk and harm. He championed greater discretion among professionals. Flanagan remarked:

> Police officers and police staff will have to use greater professional judgment, take greater risks in their decision making, and to use their discretion in order to achieve the highest levels of trust and confidence in policing. In doing so, they will have the support of their force and that there are clear and consistent standards against which their behaviour will be judged. This can be achieved by value based or principle based decision making where discretion and judgment are implemented in a way that is consistent with the values of the organisation. (Flanagan, 2008, p 53)

Flanagan (2008) suggested that individual professionalism should be reasserted with the aid of decision-making frameworks, which would then lead to officers being risk-conscious rather than risk-averse. Any new frameworks, Flanagan said, would need to be trained appropriately. Does this demonstrate what Bayley and Bittner (1984) describe as the police need to cling to the craft of policing? The police service at that time appeared to work with a number of different models, all of which attempted to provide a semblance of order to decision-making in relation to different policing situations. In 2009, there were at least six models utilised for decision-making within the police service. In relation to investigative work, CD and the MIM existed. In relation to attending incidents, there was the Conflict Management Model (CMM). This will be discussed in more detail later. Also in use was the SARA model, utilised in other fields as a decision-making model (i.e. Problem Oriented Policing; see Eck and Spelman, 1987), and trained to fledgling police officers during their probationary period (Tong et al, 2009). Third, there was the PLAN model. While not a decision-making model per se, it had at its core the idea that all police activity should be judged by core human rights considerations (James, 2016). This was later reconfigured as PLANE (to include the important aspect of ethical decision-making), and is still trained within intelligence and investigative courses in the UK (Bryant and Bryant, 2016). The

ACCESS model (Assess, Collect, Collate, Evaluate, Scrutinise and Summarise), was taught within investigative interviewing courses as a way of conducting inquiries as well as a useful means of reviewing cases for inconsistencies (Bryant, 2009a; for a fuller description, see Ede and Shepherd, 2000). Seemingly a lot of thought and effort has gone into dealing with the decision-making process within the police service.

In 2009, however, following Flanagan (2008), a paper was presented to ACPO committee encouraging the utilisation of a national decision model for operational policing (Adams, 2014). The NDM, it was suggested, would provide a national, values-based model that could be utilised whenever decisions were being made within policing (Lax, 2014). The model was described as suitable for all types of decisions, whether as a response to spontaneous incidents or within planned operations (NPIA, 2012). It has been stressed that as the model is suitable for all decisions it should be used by everyone in policing (CoP, 2016a). Having been piloted on a senior command course in 2010, and in 2012, amended as a result of feedback, the NDM was promoted nationally. It is noteworthy that some participants from the senior command course questioned why a new model was required when the conflict resolution model existed already (Adams, 2014). Once the model was adopted, steps were taken to replace references to other models such as the CMM. For instance, in the firearms manual, CMM was replaced by the NDM (Adams, 2014). APP (CoP, 2016a) provides links to the NDM within its investigation process section, and in another section entitled 'managing investigations'.

The model consists of five key stages, similar to the CMM only at the heart of the NDM when initially conceived was the concept of organisational values, as suggested by Flanagan (2008). Decisions were encouraged to be consistent with the organisational mission and values, although each police force appeared to have its own generic version of these (Lax, 2014). Table 4.1 outlines the stages of the CMM and the NDM. There appears to be little difference. However, subtle changes in relation to the NDM widen its scope to cover *any* decision-making exercise. Whether it is appropriate for all policing decisions is debatable. When the CMM was initially taught to practitioners, it was described as guidance to allow officers to determine when any force they used at incidents was proportionate, reasonable and necessary. It was also suggested that it could be used post-incident to justify actions. The CMM did not contain any review element, based on the premise that continual reassessment was necessary at *all* stages of the process. Moreover, as its name suggests, the model appeared appropriate to situations that involved conflict. However, at least one ACPO guidance document suggested that the CMM had wider utility. The document states: 'The CMM is a decision making model that is widely known and used throughout the police service. The CMM is a scaleable model that can be applied before during or after any type of planned operation or spontaneous incident, and not just to those involving conflict' (ACPO, 2009b, p 24). What is not clear is the research that supports such a contention.

The NDM specifically includes 'review', although the final stage appears to entail both action and review. Logically, one could expect there to be a sixth stage within the NDM entitled 'review' to ensure that it was undertaken separately. That said, the difference between the two models is the centrality of organisational values to the process. Officers applying the NDM were encouraged to use their professional judgement to ensure that the values of the organisation were rooted in the actions they proposed to take. Since 2014, organisational values have been replaced by the code of ethics. Decisions must now be undertaken with those core ethical principles in mind. No such principles were evident in the CMM (CoP, 2016a).

Table 4.1: Comparison between CMM and NDM

The CMM stages*	The NDM stages**
Intelligence/information	Gather information/intelligence
Threat assessment	Assess threat and risk and develop strategy
Powers/policy	Consider powers/policy
Tactical options	Identify options and contingencies
Actions	Take action and review what happened

*See ACPO, 2009b, p 24 for the model represented in a circular form

**See CoP, 2016a for the model represented in a circular form

The NDM is described as providing a simple, logical and evidence-based approach to making policing decisions (CoP, 2014a; CoP, 2016a). Evidently, the model will have the effect of reducing decision inertia and ensuring that professional discretion will be enhanced (Flanagan, 2008). Worryingly, it is suggested the NDM will support the 'appropriate' allocation of resources in an era of increasing demand. Berry (2010) champions the use of professional judgement to allow for a more victim-led, proportionate and appropriate response to incidents. The first point regarding decision inertia was accompanied by an assertion that officers would be supported by their organisation if they made reasonable decisions in the circumstances, even where the decision had a detrimental effect on others (CoP, 2016a). The IPCC similarly contended that the model reflected a positive move, explaining that they too would respect decisions made reasonably in the circumstances Encouragement for professional discretion and empowerment of officers is evident in current discourse (Curtis, 2015). Some commentators (Carson et al, 2013) suggest this is essential, particularly in relation to risk (see Chapter 7 also). The increased respect for professional discretion is in line with other forms of professional practice (Green and Gates, 2014). So too is the idea that a police officer will be judged on the basis of decisions made by peers with similar experience and rank (see, for instance, the Bolam test for medical negligence, Bolam v Friern, 1957). However, the real concern rests with the appropriate level of knowledge and understanding suitable for professional discretion (Robinson et al, 2016). Medical professionals qualify to perform their role by undertaking higher education degrees and have been immersed in the key principles that underpin their profession (e.g. medicine, science, chemistry, biology). Police officers undergo training much improved from the early days of policing, but arguably inadequate to equate to a profession. It is questionable whether the rhetoric of the organisation and the IPCC will impact decision inertia and risk aversion, even assuming that such rhetoric is realisable (Heaton, 2011). In relation to the model supporting the allocation of resources, this could be argued to conflict with the values-based nature of it. Arguably it is a way of being able to justify why particular actions were *not* undertaken on a cost-effectiveness and case importance basis. What does this mean? Are all thefts minor offences? What of the elderly pensioner who has had £10 stolen from them? What guidance exists in relation to the types of incidents where an investigator can reasonably use their discretion? In addition, a core element of any professional conduct might be assumed to be the accountability of its professionals through record-keeping. Police officers are required by law to record and retain relevant material under the auspices of CPIA. Yet CoP suggests that records made should be proportionate to the seriousness of the incident (CoP, 2016a). This is reiterated within APP also (CoP, 2016a). While encouraging professional judgement (and therefore an increase in discretionary behaviour) ACPO and CoP discourage one of the aspects likely to lead to greater accountability: the importance of record-keeping. Apart from the questionable legality of such an approach if a criminal investigation is in train, other published material suggests that it is a matter for professional judgement whether and to what extent decisions are recorded (CoP, 2016a). Carson et al (2013) also question the importance of what they call documentation as a mere covering exercise rather than as an aid to decision-making.

At all levels of criminal investigation, it has been a consistent mantra within police training that investigative decisions should be recorded, including decisions not to engage certain strategies (for instance, a decision not to use house-to-house enquiries in an investigation). In volume crime cases the recording mechanism was usually the individual officer's pocket notebook. Historically, these decisions would be transferred onto a free text section of a crime report, whereas nowadays this is entered on an electronic crime report. In serious and complex cases, an investigator will also usually record decisions on the electronic crime report. The more serious the crime, the more likely an officer is to use a policy file. This is a specific book normally used for decision-making in crimes such as kidnapping, homicide and serious sexual assaults. It can, however, be utilised for other serious or complex crime at the discretion of the investigating officer. In major crime cases, the use of a policy file is governed by Home Office Circular 12/1992 (ACPO, 2006). This states that key decisions should be recorded by an investigating officer. The lack of recorded decisions in the Stephen Lawrence murder investigation attracted much criticism. Bearing in mind the case seriousness, an inquiry found a paucity of decisions recorded by the senior officers involved in leading the initial investigation (Macpherson, 1999). Remarking on the lack of recorded decisions, particularly a decision not to arrest named suspects, the inquiry noted:

> If this decision was truly made after detailed consideration and proper consultation it should undoubtedly have been recorded in the policy file. This is not a bureaucratic requirement. The policy file must record important, and indeed vital decisions of this kind, both for record purposes, and in order to set out the thinking that the SIO has applied to the case. (Macpherson, 1999, p 122)

As with other areas of investigative practice, there is little research on either the effectiveness of the NDM or its utility for all decision-making within policing. Lax (2014) conducted a small-scale case study of the implementation of the NDM in one police force. Lax found that force values failed to permeate the organisation, and by implication, the impact of those values on the practice of decision-making were minimal. Bearing in mind that the decision model is values-based, this is problematic. The central core of the model was changed in 2014 to the code of ethics promulgated by CoP (CoP, 2014a). Building on the seven Nolan principles of public life, the code of ethics consists of nine principles including accountability, fairness, integrity, objectivity and honesty. The codes link to standards of professional behaviour and include a section supporting the use of NDM (CoP, 2014a, p 17). The codes have statutory basis, and are seen as one of the core components of the professionalisation agenda. There is evidence that the code of ethics, supported by CoP, have not been widely supported within the service, with CoP suffering from a lack of recognition within policing (House of Commons Home Affairs Committee, 2016). This is worrying, given the importance of the ethical framework in underpinning professional practice.

Is the NDM *really* suitable for all decisions in policing or is it more appropriate for operational responses to problems? Examples regarding use of NDM relate to single decisions rather than the multiplicity of decisions taken within criminal investigations (CoP, 2015, pp 10–11). There appear to be no independent studies of NDM or CMM, and what material exists by way of explanation of NDM merely set out its stages with little discussion or example as to how it fits with established detective decision-making (see, for instance, Cook and Tattersall, 2014). Criminal investigations involve a number of decisions. Even the most straightforward investigations might involve a high number. The more complex an investigation, the higher the number of decisions that will need to be made by the lead investigator or SIO. In what respect do officers need to comply with NDM for each decision? Do they all need to demonstrate compliance with the NDM? Admittedly, APP and Cook and Tattersall (2014) suggest that only important decisions need recording, and once again the idea of professional discretion is advanced as a reason why it can be left to the individual officer to decide what to record. In an era of more work and fewer resources (see Chapter 2), the default position for an overworked investigator is likely to be to record the bare minimum. Rather than encourage professional practice such woolly guidance is likely to foster unprofessional practice that only leaves individual officers vulnerable to disciplinary infringements. After all, they have been told that they will be supported if they have acted in accordance with the NDM and will be deemed to have acted reasonably if they have followed its principles. The potential effect of the NDM is far from creating less work for investigators in terms of investigations and recording mechanisms; it might do exactly the opposite.

Conclusion

The paucity of research in this very important area of investigative practice is alarming, particularly when considered against the backdrop of MOJ cases. Add to that the importance of decision-making to the gatekeeping function for admission into the criminal justice system and current high-profile examples of failure in relation to rape, domestic abuse, mental health and other vulnerability, then the importance and urgency of research is increased. There is also a pressing need to undertake research in the area of investigative decision-making models to discover answers to some very important questions. Is the NDM suitable for all decisions within policing? Is it appropriate for decision-making within criminal investigations? How does such a model currently assist investigators in decision-making within criminal investigations, particularly those that are of a serious, complex or major nature? And finally, does the notion of a thorough investigation withstand austerity and the need to utilise resources sparingly? What do the public and the authorities want and expect of investigators undertaking so-called minor crime investigations? Should there be a two-tier system relating to models of investigation? If so, how does this link to professionalism and how does this enable progression from a volume crime investigator through to an investigator of serious and complex crime?

Further reading

Lax, M. (2014) 'The affective domain and police values education: is the former used to convey the latter in support of the national decision model?' *Police Journal: Theory Practice and Principles*, 87(2): 126–38.

Nickerson, R.S. (1998) 'Confirmation bias: a ubiquitous phenomenon in many guises'. *Review of General Psychology*, 2(2): 175–220.

Rossomo, K.D. (2008) *Criminal investigative failures*. Boca Raton, FL: CRC Press.

FIVE

The centrality of law

Introduction

It is often said that there is a discord between law in action and law in
books (Newburn and Reiner, 2004), as well as the rule of law and the
reality of policing (Skolnick, 1966). The line of argument is that the
police do a very difficult job, but have often resorted to rule-bending
or using 'ways and means' to ensure that their understanding of the
term 'justice' is achieved. This may involve a range of activities, from
concentrating on one suspect to the exclusion of others, ignoring
contradictory evidence, and failing to disclose exculpatory evidence,
through to deliberately fabricating evidence to ensure conviction. The
behaviour ensures that those considered guilty receive their just deserts.
Several high-profile cases and MOJs have confirmed that the police are
not always correct when assuming guilt (i.e. Colin Stagg). There is some
suggestion of courts for many years providing tacit approval by turning
a blind eye to these types of police practices (Bayley, 2002), preferring
to allow any misdemeanours to go unpunished for the smooth and
effective running of the criminal justice system (Holdaway, 1983;
Smith and Gray, 1983; Ericson, 1993; Runciman, 1993). McConville
et al (1991) suggest that law-breaking and rule-bending is a systemic
set of practices. As an example, they suggest that new laws enacted to
curtail police misuse of power (such as PACE) were easily subsumed
into existing practices.

The modern era has seen a plethora of legislation enacted that directly
impacts on the work of detectives (Ashworth, 2000). In some cases,
the law was changed to regulate the work of detectives because high-
profile cases demonstrated abuses of power and poor decision-making
that led directly or indirectly to MOJs (Snook and Cullen, 2008). Once
uncovered, public outcry would ensue, followed by an inquiry, followed
by some form of statement from the police that lessons had been learnt,
followed by new legislation designed to curb executive power and to
protect the rights of citizens (Heaton, 2011). It is possible to trace the
development of PACE, CPIA and, to a certain extent, RIPA and the
HRA. All of these enactments directly impact on the work of the
police and criminal investigations in particular (Newburn and Reiner,

2004). It is axiomatic that an investigator would need to be aware of law in order to be able to perform their role within its confines. It is also little surprise that an investigator would need to know aspects of substantive criminal law in order to effectively investigate crimes either reported by the public or coming to their attention from elsewhere. The interesting debate is to what extent do crime investigators need to know the law, how much of it do they need to know, and how much training do they need to be provided in relation to it? Chapter 4 has highlighted the push towards a more discretionary approach to police decision-making, and tensions between such an approach and formal legal knowledge have been highlighted by Wood et al (2017). This chapter will explore senses in which the law has been used negatively or unprofessionally, ranging from flagrant breaches to manipulation. It will also consider senses in which law is central to criminal investigative practice and needs to be used by practitioners in a more developed, professional manner. While the chapter does not suggest that knowledge of law is everything to investigative practice, it does suggest that it is central to it.

Law in an unprofessional sense

We have seen how previous research criticised detective training for being focused primarily on teaching the law, even criticising it for being taught to be used as a weapon against suspects in interview (Laurie, 1970; Maguire and Norris, 1992). Morgan (1990) and Irving and Dunnighan (1993), note how police training was heavily dominated by teaching what they describe as 'technical law' and procedure. Indeed HMIC made similar criticisms in a detailed report on police training at the turn of the century (HMIC, 2002). The criticisms suggested that law training was provided at the expense of essential skills, such as communication, investigative interviewing and the use of discretion. We have already traced how training has developed within the police milieu over the last two decades, with programmes under the auspices of PIP providing specific knowledge acquisition and skills development phases. Further criticisms related to teaching officers techniques to bend or avoid the law, or to use it to manipulate suspects into providing incriminating evidence (Maguire, 2008). Maguire and Norris (1992) provide an example of a detective sergeant who claimed to have been taught how to ask questions in a way that elicited an incriminatory response from a suspect ('If I lived around here I would want to protect myself too'), manipulating a person to agree and thus satisfy the requirements of a criminal offence.

Maguire (2008) also notes how detectives used their detailed knowledge of points to prove to manipulate suspects into incriminating themselves in interview, thereby persuading them to accept that they were guilty of crime. Such interviews began with the premise that the suspect was guilty. Tong et al (2009) derided the 'points to prove' mentality and championed the ideal of a search for the truth. However, there is academic debate around what exactly the *raison d'être* of the modern criminal justice system is. Roberts (2007) suggests that a criminal justice system with an accent on due process is concentrated around the notion of legal guilt (proof not truth), while the crime control model has the dominant notion of factual guilt rather than truth. The argument runs that detectives (and maybe a large proportion of police officers) have traditionally seen their role from the perspective of crime control. In cases where they assume factual guilt but lack the evidence to prove legal guilt, officers have sometimes resorted to illegal means to ensure that the person is convicted of the crime (Holdaway, 1983). These illegal means have included 'verballing' suspects (thereby claiming that they have confessed to the crime), manipulating witnesses into providing false evidence, falsifying evidence, and deliberately ignoring evidence of an exculpatory nature (Matza, 1969; Holdaway, 1983; Brodeur, 2010).

An even more sinister connotation is the idea that police use the law as a form of coercive power and punishment outside of the system of punishments existing in the criminal justice system. In this sense, the argument runs, police exact their own kind of retribution and punishment by effecting 'summary justice' by utilising powers of arrest, searching, interrogating and stopping and searching citizens in the name of law. They do this even if they know there is little chance of a successful prosecution, because this behaviour *is* the punishment. Seen in this way, it matters little about guilt or innocence because the ends justify the means (Holdaway, 1983; Klockars, 1980) and a form of justice is exacted by that process. Such a view inclines to the notion that police officers are familiar with the law – so familiar that they can use it to manipulate situations to utilise their full powers.

All of the above practices and processes are anathema to the rule of law (Dicey, 1959; Bingham, 2011) and have rightly been subject to criticism and action when they have been uncovered. However, it is the nature of police work where decisions are made in circumstances often without scrutiny, that these very dangers exist (Newburn and Reiner, 2004). Critics argue that the reasoning behind many of these practices stems from the fact that the police believe they *know* that a suspect is guilty (Klockars, 1980). Because they have such a belief: they have knowledge of the individual (perhaps they have dealt with them in the past, or they have knowledge of their individual circumstances), the law is not satisfactory in helping them convict the obviously guilty and bring them to justice, so it is all right (in their view) to inconvenience them or cause them angst in the form of summary justice, or in a manipulative way to get them to admit offences (Klockars, 1980; Brodeur, 2010).

So, the law can be utilised in a negative manner, allowing police to justify abusing citizens' rights (Klockars, 1980). It can also be used to restrict access to the criminal justice system (Goldstein, 1960) in the sense of a 'policeman as expert', informing a victim that the behaviour of a suspect does not fit the criterion of a criminal offence or the matter is a 'civil' debt in which the police are powerless to intervene (Patrick, 2011a, 2011b). These preceding ideas are based on the premise that the police deliberately use the law to support inaction when in fact the law could be utilised. Often such decisions are made in circumstances of low visibility and are not open to scrutiny (Goldstein, 1960).

Another example might extend to cases where police dissuade complainants from continuing with a criminal investigation by informing them that an essential ingredient of the offence reported to them is missing, meaning that a prosecution is unlikely. Effectively, a complainant is misled into thinking that the points to prove of an offence have not been satisfied, and therefore withdraws their complaint (see, for instance, allegations that police routinely talked rape and serious sexual assault complainants out of reporting crimes by suggesting that the essential element of non-consent was lacking [IPCC, 2013a]). New Home Office Counting Rules (Home Office, 2016) disavow this practice, as well as the practice of investigating a report (without formally recording it as a crime) until such time as regarded as valid. According to new rules, crimes should be recorded if, on the balance of probabilities, they satisfy the definition of a relevant criminal offence, something which the police will need to decide calling on their knowledge of the law (Home Office, 2016). Patrick (2011a), however, identifies how police will shift the burden of proof to a crime victim to establish that a crime has been committed to ensure that fewer crimes are recorded. Law can also be used as leverage in police interactions with citizens in the sense of threats made to invoke the law unless a person provides information about the criminal activities of others. Sometimes such activities are sanctioned (see, for instance, the Serious Organised Crime and Police Act 2005 (SOCPA) provisions relating to offenders assisting prosecutions), but on many occasions are not visible or open to scrutiny (Bayley and Bittner, 1984).

None of the above examples include even more flagrant breaches of the law where police officers deliberately break the law in order to ensure that a suspect is found guilty (see, for instance, the West Midlands Crime Squad scandal of the 1980s). Again, this type of behaviour is usually predicated on the false assumption that the suspect *must* be guilty of the offence for which they are under investigation (Skolnick, 1966; Sanders, 1977; Holdaway, 1983; Maguire and Norris, 1992). These notions are also distinguishable from the more benign rule-breaking and failure to adhere to policy highlighted by Innes (2003) in the term 'compliance drift', connoting behaviour that, while accompanied by less sinister motives, can nevertheless become fatal to the outcome of a case at a later point and still potentially cause MOJs.

Skolnick (1966) identified how detectives in the USA distinguished between substantive law that defined the nature and extent of criminal offences, and procedural law that defined the limits of police powers within investigations. He observed that detectives felt there was a moral distinction that could be drawn in relation to breaking these different types of law. As an example, if anyone broke the criminal law (even a police officer), officers felt that investigation, charge and conviction was justified. This was morally correct in their eyes. However, they felt differently about procedural laws designed (in their view) to put obstacles in the way of their crime-fighting remit. They did not feel it was morally wrong to breach procedural laws in order to secure convictions against people they knew were guilty. Assuming knowledge of a suspect's guilt is a trait in police investigators that has been found throughout the world, including the UK (Skolnick, 1966; Klockars, 1980; McConville et al, 1981; Holdaway, 1983; Maguire and Norris, 1992), although there is little current research available about modern investigators. On a more positive note, Maguire and Norris do note that in their 1992 study, investigators appeared to be less wedded to the notion of conviction at all costs, and were more comfortable with PACE because they had only worked in the post-PACE era since they had joined the police service. O'Neill (2011) asked volume crime investigators why MOJs occurred. Interestingly, some felt that they were no longer a facet of modern investigations, a somewhat naïve perspective. They also valued knowledge of the law as less important to effective investigative work than traits such as determination, conscientiousness, communication and decision-making skills. They valued education even less, ranking it the lowest of 30 skills, abilities and characteristics. This may reflect the cultural ambivalence towards education and training and the craft mentality (Bayley and Bittner, 1984). Roberts (2007) recognised the importance of law to criminal investigations. He suggested that the law serves to structure criminal investigations in two ways – first by clarifying the specific objectives of investigations, and second by seeking to regulate the conduct of those involved in them. Criminal law, he says, defines the elements of a criminal offence, thus providing what proof is required in order to secure a criminal conviction. These criminal offences in police vernacular would be simplified in the form of 'points to prove'. They can act to frame the focus of investigations.

Law in a professional sense

There are several ways in which knowledge of the law is fundamental to effective investigations. In the first instance, there is wide discretion afforded to each individual police officer in terms of how, when and whether to act when faced with a breach of the criminal law (see Blackburn, 1968). That said, modern police officers are bound to act in most cases for fear of being subjected to disciplinary procedures for neglect of duty if they ignore obvious offences (Hough, 2013), and the advent of the CPS has ensured that prosecutorial decision making is out of the hands of the police. On the other hand, much police discretion by its very nature is less visible and therefore unaccountable. Wood et al (2017), recognise the tension between discretion and legal knowledge, and suggest that over-reliance on legal knowledge fails to equip officers for the realities of policing. They do not, however, suggest that knowledge of the law is unnecessary, merely that on its own it is insufficient for effective practice, particularly when discretion plays a major part. It will be interesting to see how much protection an officer is afforded if they use their discretion not to invoke the law in certain circumstances. This might be in conjunction with the new NDM, applying a reasonable approach to resolving an issue rather than invoking the full weight of the law. Nobody expects a police officer to be a walking law library (do they?) and of course this must be considered when making ex post facto judgements as to the reasonableness of an officer's conduct. However, the public would be entitled to expect a modern professional police officer to be able to distinguish whether conduct, first, amounts to a criminal offence and, second, whether they feel it is appropriate to act on it in a proportionate manner that might not involve utilising full police powers. Therein lie some of the dangers of discretion. Not only can it be applied to a situation in a wrongful manner, applying a discriminatory, judgemental or biased approach, it can be applied incorrectly if an officer is either ignorant of the law, has a lack of understanding of it or simply applies it incorrectly to a real-life situation.

Discretion is dangerous if applied *without* knowledge of the law. Current rhetoric encourages officers to use their resourcefulness in resolving issues without recourse to the law, seemingly leaning towards a compliance rather than sanctioning approach (Ashworth, 2000). Arguably, this is not such a bad approach, especially when much of what occurs is trivial in nature and when according to research such as Maguire and Norris (1992) the proportion of incidents that involve crime is low (Ashworth, 2000; Hough, 2013; CoP, 2016a). It is also a pragmatic response to finite resources (Lustgarten, 1987). A few issues arise with this position. First, too much discretion inevitably leads to a lack of consistency in application of the law and unequal treatment (Lustgarten, 1987; Ashworth, 2000). Moreover, it still requires the decision-maker to consider the law (Lustgarten, 1987). This is irrespective of whether a proportionate response is favoured where prosecution is the last resort (Ashworth, 2000; Brodeur, 2010; Hough, 2013). Robinson and Tilley (2009) suggest that a discretionary approach requires at the very least competent, experienced and well-motivated officers. Competence would, by necessity, require sound legal knowledge. Second, Maguire and Norris (1992) found that 25% of police time was spent dealing with crime, with 75% dealing with miscellaneous incidents not considered to be crimes. More recently, Greater Manchester Police (GMP), with a clear agenda, identified that one third of callers to their 999 system reported crimes, while the remaining two thirds related to what they described as 'social work'. In the social work category, they included alcohol-related disturbances, missing persons, relationship disputes and mental health issues (Brogden and Ellison, 2013). Such statistics may serve to understate the number of times a police officer will have to engage their knowledge of the law in order to consider what their response to a situation is. In a majority of calls, from missing persons, to missing patients, to neighbour disputes, to obstruction of a driveway to sudden deaths, police officers will need to engage in consideration of the legal nature of an interaction, and the proportional legally justified response to it. First classification of a call or even final classification of a call might not identify whether a police officer was taxed with having to think about their legal powers or whether they resolved a situation without doing so. The HMIC have suggested that as many as 80% of calls relate to potential rather than actual crime incidents (HMIC, 2012), although there are discrepancies between different studies with estimations of between 5% and 80% of police incidents being said to 'involve' crime (Brodeur, 2010). Bayley and Bittner (1984) once determined that at a domestic abuse call, police officers could take at least nine different courses of action on contact with the individuals involved. They then calculated at least 11 potential processing tactics, and a further 11 exit strategies (including arrest of a suspect). Many of the considerations involved by implication the considerations of legal powers, and in the UK the attendance at the call would satisfy the definition of a criminal investigation (CPIA, 1996a, 1996b) Another problematic consideration is that a case resolved as 'no further action' or where so-called 'common sense' has prevailed does not necessarily mean that a call has been dealt with appropriately or lawfully. If a suspect is arrested for this crime or any other, the range of considerations could become fewer, although this would be an interesting area of study in modern investigative practice. We have looked at the sense in which law can (and has been) used by the police in a negative, aggressive and illegal manner. But what are the senses in which the law can be and has been used in a more positive, constructive way?

Law to inform practice

Officers' attitudes to learning and the reality of policing is well rehearsed (Roberts, 2007; Sanders and Young, 2006; Tong and Wood, 2011). Indeed, it has prompted observers to identify a marked difference between law in books and law in action – the rhetoric of law vs its application in reality. While much has been discussed by previous research around cultural resistance of police officers to training that they feel is abstract from reality, little has been researched around the nature and quality of police legal training in the UK. Law taught in abstract would be much more difficult to comprehend if not trained in a practical manner, stressing the impact that each piece of legislation or case law has on everyday practice. Investigators at all levels are challenged with actual or potential criminal investigations. Some are asked to attend an incident where they will need to determine what has happened, whether there may be potential for a criminal offence to have been committed, and what if any action is appropriate and proportionate to the situation (the third point relates to the much-discussed area of police discretion). As Roberts (2007, p 98) suggests: 'Legal definitions of criminal offences are also highly salient to the early stages of criminal investigation, long before courtroom litigation is a prospect.' Maguire (2008) suggests that legal knowledge is one of the most important skills of a detective in practice, although whether this amounts to a 'skill' is debatable.

We have already identified the situation of a police officer being called to a death on a building site (Chapter 1). On arrival, the police officer (a patrol officer with limited police service, but nevertheless an investigator as defined by the CPIA) will use their training and knowledge to consider what to do in relation to the parties at the location (potential witnesses), and the dead body. The police officer will have much to consider in this scenario. Even though officers may believe (prematurely) that this is unlikely to be a crime at this point, they will need to consider material that may assist a coroner to decide on the cause of death (as a minimum). In addition, the police officer will know that there are several policies, procedures and practices that will need to be followed in order to respond appropriately.

Issues that will be important for the officer will be:

- management of the place where the person died (potentially a crime scene at this point);
- management of witnesses;
- interaction with witnesses;
- the search for relevant evidence;
- procedural issues in relation to liaison with other officers who might attend, for instance, supervisors or members of the detective branch.

Assuming the first response does little more than maintain the scene, these same considerations now fall to the officer more senior in rank or the detective officer who attends. But even in scene maintenance, the officer will need to understand fully the extent of their legal powers to retain it.

Moreover, first responders will need to consider conflict management, victim and witness welfare and the identification of risk. They may also need to make several decisions in relation to these matters. We have seen in Chapter 4 how the police service currently encourages its officers to utilise the NDM (the value based decision model). One of the five stages of that model contemplates consideration of policies and legal powers (CoP, 2016a). This necessitates consideration of the legal aspects of the situation and any actions that the officer chooses to make.

Which of the professionals in this scenario can afford to attend a scene such as this with little or no knowledge of both substantive and procedural law? While nobody expects the police officer to be an expert, they might expect them, as modern professionals, to have a good understanding of what possibilities exist in relation to culpability for death, despite the fact that the outcome of the investigation might find no fault at all. Additionally, the police officer will need to be cognisant of powers to search, powers to seize potential evidence, powers to erect a police cordon, powers to arrest, as well as the limits and restrictions on these powers. That is so even if they do not use those powers, and even if they decide to utilise them proportionately as they are encouraged to do.

As can be seen from the foregoing discussion of the death on the building site, knowledge of law can have a direct and positive effect on the practice of policing, assuming that response is appropriate. Rather than being irrelevant, law is a form of evidence-based practice, allowing a police officer to act in a manner currently proscribed by statute, codes of practice and common law. Any professional practice needs to ensure that professionals within it not only acquire that knowledge, but also have facilities available to them to allow them to access the very latest material that informs that practice (Runciman, 1993). We have seen that modern investigators are trained in elements of the law, depending on the programme and level of study they have undertaken. To qualify as a detective, distance learning is utilised for the law, with a multiple choice national examination testing knowledge. Other parts of the programme concentrate on skill development with little time to blend law and practice. Officers are kept up to date with legal developments by CoP digests, internal training (if provided), e-learning, and access to the Police National Legal Database. The effectiveness of many of these sources is under-researched.

To utilise another example where problems of proof often arise, take a report of rape by a drunk female. A woman has contacted police to say that she has been raped. She tells police that she went to a nightclub with friends but was split up from them. She did not see them again. She states she met a man in the nightclub, got talking to him, and had a number of drinks and dances with him. She remembers that they left the nightclub together, in the early hours, and walked along a road. She was drunk, and remembers she had been sick in both the nightclub and the street as they walked along a footpath. She cannot remember all the evening or the events after she left the nightclub, only that the man said he would walk her home. She had a poor memory of what happened next, but does remember at one point the man pulling up her dress and penetrating her with his penis. She states that she would never have given her consent to this activity but could not remember whether she had resisted or said anything.

Notwithstanding common myths, judgemental attitudes and discriminatory practices that sometimes accompany these types of investigations (Temkin and Krahé, 2008), let us assume that an investigator begins this investigation keen to investigate thoroughly and objectively in order to determine what has happened. What is an investigator to do in these circumstances? Some officers might consider that it is already a difficult task, there probably being no witnesses to the encounter. Of course, this is an assumption until investigative activity has taken place. At the beginning of any report, investigators need to be acutely aware of their responsibilities to investigate in a fair and objective manner (Henriques, 2016). Chapter 4 discussed the dangers of making judgements too early. The earlier judgements are made (without evidence to support them) the more likely conclusions will be incorrect and cases fail. However, academic literature contains examples of police investigations defaulting to a position of blame *against* a complainant, particularly when they are deemed to have failed to live up to perceptions of an ideal victim (Christie, 1986).

The scenario provided does not appear to conform to a stereotypical rape scenario. In fact, most real-life rape scenarios do not conform to the stereotype. That is, perpetrated by a stranger, dressed in black, jumping out of the bushes and attacking a lone female with a knife (Temkin and Krahé, 2008). This stereotypical situation would usually happen at night, the female would scream, put up a fight, suffer injury and then be overpowered. This is a myth for many reasons. A large majority of rapes are committed by people known to the victim. Sometimes these are close friends and intimate partners. Some victims freeze with fright and are thus unable to struggle (Mason and Lodrick, 2013). Some acquiesce for fear of being killed or significantly harmed. Whatever the type of case, absence of injury is not evidence that the person was not raped. Some victims are male. They will often be affected in similar ways to female victims, although not always. The fact that the person was voluntarily drunk does not mean they were responsible for their plight, despite judicial comment on that fact recently (*Guardian*, 2017). People have the freedom to get drunk – it is not a crime to do so unless it manifests itself in some form of criminality such as public order, assaults, driving offences or incapacity. The unfortunate consequence of the rape myth is that many in society are brought up to believe it. First, offenders may not consider that their conduct constitutes rape, because it does not conform to that stereotype. Second, victims may believe the stereotype too, and might not therefore consider what happened to them constitutes rape. They may never report the matter to police, or they do so some time after it has occurred. Police officers are drawn from society. Some of them might also believe that the only real rape is a stranger rape. Consequently, when a complainant reports a rape outside this scenario, the investigator might approach it with a negative attitude (i.e. this is not a *real* rape). Their response and their subsequent investigation may therefore be sub-standard and less thorough. The non-conformist reports will encompass cases such as those above, marital rapes, rapes committed by friends, work colleagues, partners, and cases where a person is in an alleged position of trust (i.e. taxi driver). The challenge for modern investigators is to investigate thoroughly *first* before jumping to rash conclusions about the nature of the incident reported and either guilt or innocence of a suspect (Henriques, 2016).

The law in relation to consent is contained in the Sexual Offences Act 2003 (Stevenson, 2004; Ormerod and Laird, 2015). Our example deals with a complaint of rape, but the case law discussed and consent issues are relevant to all four non-consensual sexual offences in the Act (That is, rape, assault by penetration, sexual assault and causing sexual activity without consent). Consent is defined in section 74 of the act to encompass agreement by choice providing a person has the requisite freedom and capacity to choose (Ormerod and Laird, 2015). The Act also provides examples of situations (known as presumptions), where in certain circumstances it may be presumed by a court that there was no consent, or reasonable belief in consent (Section 75 and 76 Sexual Offences Act 2003). Examples of s75 include where violence is used or threatened, or where they are being held captive against their will. In these cases, non-consent will be assumed by the court unless the defendant can raise an issue as to the existence of consent to such activity in those circumstances (i.e. sado-masochistic practices). The issue of drunkenness was not specifically listed in any of the presumptions, leaving this to be decided on a case-by-case basis in relation to the general definition in section 74. Some commentators criticised the law for being too imprecise, while others criticised it for not specifically adding victim drunkenness to the list of presumptions (Rook and Ward, 2014). Then Home Secretary David Blunkett reasoned that they did not want too many 'mischievous accusations', which they envisaged if the proposed clause was included (BBC, 2006). Section 74 of the Sexual Offences Act is thus the main section where arguments relating to drunken consent occur. The section appears to cover situations where a victim does not consent, together with situations where a victim cannot consent. A person does not consent in situations where they do not agree to the activity, whether they actually express that disagreement or not (they do not in short have to say no; in fact this would be too high a position to take, especially when we already know that some people freeze and say nothing through fear, while some may be compliant for similar reasons (R v Bree, 2007). So these people do not agree by choice, and in some cases, it can be argued that they do not have the freedom to do so. Section 74 makes clear that freedom, capacity and choice need to be present for consent. In the absence of any one of these, no consent is present. On the other hand, some people may not have capacity to consent because they are unconscious, asleep, too drunk or under the influence of drugs, or because they have particular mental or physical disabilities (Ormerod and Laird, 2015). The law was unclear on exactly the position when a person (the victim) had voluntarily consumed so much alcohol that they were drunk. Did this mean that a person could not then consent to sexual activity? Did this mean that a person engaging in sexual activity with a drunk person was committing a non-consensual sexual offence? Even if the person who has consumed the alcohol had consented? Often people who want to do something (not just sexual activity) might steel themselves to do it by consuming alcohol. In an important Court of Appeal judgement, the court in R v Bree (2007) set out some clarity in relation to drunkenness and consent. Ruling in this case that the defendant Bree should have his conviction quashed, the court made three significant points. First, a person does not have to say 'No' for circumstances to amount to rape. There are numerous situations where this is either impossible or the victim feels unable to do so. Second, the court stated that it would be impossible to identify a specific number of drinks that would identify when a person was too drunk to consent, because every person is different in terms their constitution (weight, size and tolerance to alcohol). Third, the court reiterated that drunken consent could be consent. However, they also made it clear that there would be circumstances where a person consumes so much that they would be incapable of giving consent, and therefore section 74 of the Sexual Offences Act would apply. The courts anticipated that someone who was too drunk would be incapable of consenting to sexual activity. Anyone engaging in sexual activity with them at that point would be committing a sexual offence if all other elements of the offence were present. The effect of this case, on a practical level for investigations, was that where incapacity through drink or drugs was at issue, the investigation would need to provide a thorough and detailed evidential picture of a complainant's physical state at the time the incident took place. Police would need to build a picture to demonstrate that the person was not only drunk but too drunk. It must be stressed that this relates to drink or drug consumption. Where a report is that a person did not consent because they were incapable of doing so, then investigative effort would be required to determine whether the evidence supported or refuted that proposition. This type of case reflects non-consent through incapacity as opposed to non-consent for other reasons (for example fear, deception, threats, assaults or blackmail). CPS advice on cases where capacity to consent is in issue suggests: 'Prosecutors and investigators should consider whether supporting evidence is available to demonstrate that the complainant was so intoxicated that he/she had lost their capacity to consent. For example, evidence from friends, taxi drivers and forensic physicians describing the complainant's intoxicated state may support the prosecution case' (CPS, 2017).

Cases like Bree (2007) demonstrate that good knowledge and understanding of both legislation and case law can inform investigative process and focus. Moreover, assuming that the investigator has found the required evidence of either no consent or an inability to consent, following completion of their investigation, they would be required to submit the evidence to a specialist rape lawyer (RASSO) for a charging decision. That case file should reflect the basis on which lack of consent is asserted, with the evidence to support it. Anecdotal evidence suggests that inclusion of relevant case law and legislation in support of a submission can have a positive effect, particularly if the prosecutor is unaware (in exceptional circumstances) of a particular stated case. Additionally, a recent joint HMIC and HMCPSI inspection (HMIC and HMCPSI, 2013), suggested that police summaries of evidence lacked essential proof for the points to prove. Knowledge of the effect of common law cases assists in the submission of evidentially sound, professional case files.

In any area of investigative practice, whether at volume or major crime level, investigators will be required to make decisions that turn on issues of substantive or procedural law (Stelfox, 2009). The NDM, encourages officers to consider the legality of their actions (Cook and Tattersall, 2014). This cannot be done without sound knowledge of the law. As Runciman (1993) suggested, not only should professional practice have the requisite training, it should also have an accent on continuing professional development to ensure that practitioners are up to date with the latest developments that affect practice. We have already seen that the police national evaluation of PIP identified the CPD element of the process to be one of the poorest aspects of its current process and in need of development (CoP, 2014b), and work is underway to improve this situation, albeit surprisingly late (CoP, 2016a). Not only will knowledge of the law inform investigative practice, it provides investigative focus.

Legal knowledge is also required throughout an investigation (Stelfox, 2009). As discussed in Chapter 1, principles of CPIA are essential for practice, bearing in mind that they not only regulate disclosure, but also duties to record, retain and reveal material, as well as the very process of investigation. If an officer wishes to pursue surveillance, mount observations or engage in proactive work of any kind, they will need to ensure that they have the requisite knowledge of RIPA and its associated codes of practice (and the new Investigatory Powers Act [IPA], 2016). While forces usually provide good advice and guidance to investigators in relation to these matters, and the legal considerations to be applied, investigators must be alert to the potential for their use within their investigations.

It is essential for investigators to understand the legal footing on which they undertake interviews of suspects and witnesses. The intricacies of PACE and the safeguard of individual rights are enshrined within this and other legislation (Bull, 2014). Detailed knowledge of the limits of suspicion, the reasonableness of grounds to arrest, the necessity to arrest and the use of urgent interviews are all integral to a professional approach to investigation, as are the limits of data protection and disclosure of information to the public in exceptional circumstances. All these powers are required to be exercised with good judgement, reasonably, proportionately, and in compliance with the Human Rights Act.

When planning and preparing interviews, investigators must consider what potential offences there might be under investigation (Shepherd and Griffiths, 2013). At the beginning of the interview they are required to make it clear to a suspect what the nature of the investigation is (Police and Criminal Evidence Act [PACE], 1984). They could not, for instance, tell them that they are investigating a minor assault when a person has died – they must tell them the nature of the offences they are suspected of. In addition, in order to conduct a thorough and professional interview, investigators are encouraged to plan and prepare by considering the offences under investigation. By including this within their interview plan, investigators should be able to judge whether there are any questions to identify whether the person's actions amount to a particular offence or not. This is not concerned with obtaining confession evidence, as the emphasis of police suspect interviews has changed significantly over time (Clarke and Milne, 2001). The reason is to ensure that relevant questions have been identified in the planning and preparation stage, and asked of the suspect, thereby ensuring that they have been given an opportunity to answer.

Since 2003, the Criminal Justice Act has allowed relevant evidence that constitutes bad character to be used against a defendant. This is strictly controlled by the legislation, with a number of gateways for the admissibility of different types of bad character evidence. The intention of the legislation was to assist in the evidence-based conviction of people who, by the facts of the case and the admission of relevant bad character, were clearly guilty (R v Hanson, Gilmore and Pickstone, 2005). The interview provides an opportunity for an investigator to ask questions about relevant previous behaviour. The investigator will therefore need to have a sound understanding of the principles of bad character, the use that can be made of it in criminal cases, and how it might be utilised within interviews.

Investigators at every level must be aware of legal duties they have in relation to members of the public when they are undertaking investigations, particularly in circumstances where authorities become aware that a person's life is in immediate danger (Osman v United Kingdom, 1998). They must assess the threat level to a person and put protective measure in place when they believe that the threat level is high (Brookman and Innes, 2013). Lately, domestic abuse threats have received attention and most forces have been applying a risk assessment tool known as Domestic Abuse Stalking and Harassment (DASH) in order to try to identify the level of threat that may exist for a DA victim (Ariza et al, 2016). Whether this has been a successful strategy is open to debate, designed as it is to protect the lives of particularly vulnerable individuals (see Chapter 7 for further discussion).

At some point in a criminal investigation, at any level, the police may be required to formulate a form of case theory and provide a file of evidence to the CPS for consideration. Points to prove, used in the sense of assisting investigative focus, evidence-based rather than formed from early assumptions of guilt, are ultimately important to the presentation of the evidence to the CPS (McConville et al, 1991; Innes, 2003; Stelfox and Pease, 2005; Roberts, 2007; HMIC and HMCPSI, 2013). Each crime has elements that need to be proven before criminal liability can ensue (Ashworth, 2000; Roberts, 2007). A recent joint HMIC and HMCPSI review of police case files (2013) found 63% of police MG5s (summary of evidence) deficient in a number of areas. One of those areas related to proving a case and setting out the points to prove. The expectation from prosecutors is that this is provided by the police, although this was not evident in the files reviewed. The joint review recommended that CoP provide extra training and education to police officers in substantive and procedural law, suggesting a shortfall somewhere. However it is expressed, providing a case file with relevant evidence *is* case construction, and is a necessary part of the process. The real danger of case construction lies in the point at which investigators decide that they 'know' who is responsible, or where they decide that particular pieces of information are concrete (Fahsing and Ask, 2016). If this comes too early it leads investigators to concentrate on the wrong pool of suspects (i.e. the Yorkshire Ripper, Stagg). See also recent discussions about the belief culture of rape investigations that arguably serve to reverse the burden of proof against suspects (Henriques, 2016).

As many commentators have suggested, case-building by investigators is perhaps one of the most undervalued, even by detectives themselves who are apt to see it as a waste of valuable time that could be spent on more important investigative tasks (Hobbs, 1988; Sanders, 1977). Moreover, it has been suggested that paperwork is very important, demanding a high level of knowledge and skill, because it is crucial for the successful disposal of a case (Hobbs, 1988; Stelfox, 2009; O'Neill, 2011). In Brodeur's (2010) study, detectives described their role as more akin to courtroom evidence managers than crime solvers, and in the sense that they will have to fulfil this role once a suspect has been charged, a significant amount of preparatory legal effort is required (Innes, 2003; Brookman and Innes, 2015. While Innes (2003) discusses this phenomenon in relation to homicide detectives, all cases likely to proceed towards a criminal justice process will require a similar amount of effort. Despite Innes's (2003) observation that criminal investigation is more constructive than descriptive, by its very nature it must be the case. As Brodeur (2010) points out, once again, this area of the detective task (building a case for court) is perhaps one of the least researched areas of investigative work. Yet to be effective, it must require a sound understanding of both substantive and procedural law. As Innes states: 'The requirements of criminal law and criminal procedure then are embedded in police constructions of successful investigators' (Innes, 2003, p 297). He posits that modern homicide investigators seek to ensure that a case is not only evidentially sound, but that it is legally robust enough to withstand challenges at a future time.

Conclusion

This chapter considered the importance of law and legal knowledge to the practice of criminal investigations. Rather than something that practitioners learn in the abstract, detailed knowledge of both substantive and procedural law are essential to effective practice. Not just in the manner in which such knowledge assists an officer to construct a case, but in the manner in which it assists in defining the focus of investigation and due process requirements. This is not to suggest that skills of investigation are unimportant, but to redress a balance that appears in the literature implying that the training of law is somehow inappropriate for modern investigators. Rather, these different facets complement each other – neither can stand alone in importance in undertaking effective investigations. Without good interpersonal skills, valuable information and focus can be lost. However, through a lack of knowledge of substantive and procedural law, what is found may be ruled inadmissible at court, and cases may not receive the attention that they deserve. Commentators have linked the dominance of legal training of investigators to the negative ways in which it has sometimes been used to fulfil a crime control mandate. This chapter eschews such practices and proffers a more professional and practical approach to both legislation and case law. The PIP process allows volume crime investigators to qualify to perform their role. Usually the qualification is by undertaking a training programme. PIP level two detectives must qualify to conduct serious and complex investigations by way of the ICIDP, a programme split into three phases. Phase one contains the knowledge acquisition stage. This encompasses self-directed study, e-learning, and the requirement to pass the national examination. The following two phases involve skills acquisition and workplace assessment. It remains to be seen whether the knowledge acquisition phase equips detectives with the appropriate level of knowledge to enable them to practice effectively. An examination of IPCC reports in high-profile cases would suggest that lack of knowledge or training is a significant factor in failed cases (see Chapter 7). No independent studies exist on this important area. Moreover, the consistently neglected CPD stage of the process, essential for professional practice, needs some urgent independent reassessment. Roberts (2007, p 123) has suggested: 'Police training should aspire to inculcate in officers an appreciation of the laws which govern their professional conduct and to inspire their allegiance to the ideal of democratic policing under the rule of law.' This should be in addition to substantive law and evidence that affects daily investigative practice. A further area of investigative practice found to involve unethical and illegal practices relates to measurements of success within criminal investigations. The notions of investigative success are wrapped up in ideas of both organisational and individual success. The following chapter discusses these concepts and seeks to determine what modern notions of success look like.

Further reading

Ormerod, D. and Laird, K. (2015) *Smith and Hogan's Criminal Law*, 14th edn. Oxford: Oxford University Press.

Roberts, P. (2007) 'Law and criminal investigation'. In Newburn, T., Williamson, T. and Wright, A. (eds) *Handbook of Criminal Investigation*, pp 92–145. Cullompton, Devon: Willan Publishing.

Temkin, J., and Krahé, B. (2008) *Sexual Assault and the Justice Gap: A Question of Attitude*. London: Bloomsbury Publishing.

SIX

The problem of success

Introduction

Shadows of scandal, injustice and failed investigations have fallen on police investigative practice. Attempts to identify root causes have often concluded that it is a complex mixture of individual and organisational failings (see, for instance, IPCC reports and recommendations, Chapter 7). The added difficulty is that failings in one case can be multiple rather than singular. In 1993, the RCCJ stated that the ideal measure of police performance in criminal investigations should be quality rather than quantity. The RAND study found that thoroughness in investigation increased conviction rates (Greenwood et al, 1977). However, since the RCCJ suggestion, there has been considerable debate around the notion of success. (Reiner, 1998; Neyroud, 2008; Maguire, 2008; Tong et al, 2009; Stelfox, 2009; Brookman and Innes 2013; Gorby, 2013). The debate is complicated by differing views of what constitutes success. For instance, uniformed officers, detectives and senior officers will have differing perspectives, as might politicians, victims, victims' families and other agencies within the criminal justice system (Brookman and Innes, 2013). There is also the distinction between organisational success and individual success. All this is against the backdrop of criticism alleging that if measures of success relate to quantitative output only (i.e. detections), then the investigation processes will necessarily focus on easy-to-solve crimes to ensure that police figures are portrayed in a favourable light (Maguire and Norris, 1994; Chatterton, 2008). If an organisation chases detections in this manner, it tends to focus on easy-to-solve and major crime, leaving a large lacuna at the centre of crime and criminality that never receives the attention it deserves (Steer, 1980). This can be described as a bypassed criminal element, representing those sections of society who make a living from low-level crime but manage to stay under the radar of investigation (Steer, 1980; Chatterton, 2008; Stelfox, 2009). Moreover, any quantitative fixation risks damaging the *quality* of the output, and there is evidence that this produces gaming practices by the police (Patrick, 2011a). Reiner (1998), observes that criminal investigation is perhaps easier to measure in terms of performance than, for instance, routine patrol work. At least criminal investigation has a recognisable end product in terms of bringing someone to justice (Reiner, 1998). Whether that is as simple a distinction as it sounds is an interesting issue worthy of consideration. In 2010, targets were removed by the Home Secretary Theresa May (Curtis, 2015). This chapter will consider performance measurements in relation to criminal investigations. The historical perspective will be detailed, with focus on both organisational and individual measures of success. This will lead to a discussion of the modern perspective, where seemingly a more nuanced and sophisticated understanding of success is emerging in the academic literature. Whether such an understanding has been or is being put into practice will also be considered.

Traditional measures

The traditional measurement of police effectiveness (both organisational and individual) has been the detection rate or clear-up rate (Runciman, 1993; Reiner, 1998). Police are often criticised for their lack of effectiveness in detecting crime (Greenwood et al, 1977; Bottomley and Coleman, 1981; Burrows and Tarling, 1987), yet an illusion of success can be created by managing the books well enough (Manning, 2007). The measurement of effectiveness through the clear-up rate has been the staple of policing since the New Public Management agenda of the 1980s and 1990s (Tong et al, 2009; Patrick, 2011a). Once such targets were introduced, there is evidence that tactics were used by the police to ensure that the figures were better than they should be. There is evidence that these tactics continue in the modern era too (Patrick, 2011a), indicating the dangers of utilising only this criterion to measure police effectiveness.

Members of the public might assume that a crime is cleared up if an offender is caught, charged with a crime and subsequently convicted at court. However, the reality is more complicated than that, and somewhat easier for the police to solve crime. Home Office Circular 17/1993 set out 12 ways by which a crime could be detected or cleared up (Tong, 2005). These included: where an offender was charged or summonsed for a criminal offence; where an individual had taken an offence into consideration at court (TIC); where an offender had been proceeded against in another force area or court for an offence on that area; where an offender had been cautioned for an offence; where an offender had committed the offence but had died or was mentally ill; where an essential witness or complainant had died before court; where a victim or witness refused or was unable to attend court; where the suspect admitted the offence but it was considered there was no useful purpose in taking the case to court; or where the offence had been committed by a person under the age of criminal responsibility. The latest Outcome Framework published in the Home Office Counting Rules (Home Office, 2016), contained no less than 22 outcomes. As well as those already discussed, further criteria now exist, such as a CPS decision that it is not in the public interest to prosecute an offender (Home Office, 2016). While it is clear that there are many potential outcomes, none of the criteria take into account convictions at court. The 22 criteria imply that an investigation has come to a natural conclusion (either by way of action against the perpetrator or where there is no action for various reasons, despite the perpetrator being discovered or a case being referred or pending). As Tong (2005) remarked, when discussing the earlier version, such measures are based purely on the *outcome* of a case. It takes little account of the *process* used by an investigator, nor does it take account of the complexity of the case or its seriousness. In Home Office statistics, a theft of a bar of chocolate counts as one detection, as does a murder, yet the resources required to investigate each crime are entirely different. The practice of 'skewing', concentrating on easy-to-solve cases at the expense of more serious crime (Patrick, 2011a,b), is predictably something that will happen if all crimes, when detected, carry equal weighting. So too will other 'gaming' practices emerge, such as the unethical collection of TICs (Patrick, 2011b).

Measurement of organisational success

Criticism of the use of the detection rate to measure police effectiveness focuses on the fact that this places crime control at the heart of policing, an issue that many dispute (Curtis, 2015). There is a wealth of material to suggest that crime control per se is only a small part of the role the police perform (Brodeur, 2010). Tracing the development of measures of police performance, Neyroud (2008) notes the shifting perspective between the crime control and community models, which serve to manoeuvre performance measurement towards the prevailing model. Often priorities and objectives are politically driven and dependent on the particular crime narrative of the government of the day. A classic example of this is the government White Paper *Justice for all* (Home Office, 2001a). The government set out its intention to redress the balance of the Criminal Justice System in favour of the victim, and to provide the police service with the facilities to bring more offenders to justice. Part of this new process was to ensure a greater number of detections through police reform and the provision of more skilled investigators. The government wanted police to: 'Prevent and reduce crime and deal with all aspects when a crime does occur–investigate, arrest, detain, appear as expert witnesses in court and provide a high quality of care to victims and witnesses' (Home Office, 2001a, p 6).

While it has been suggested that the use of targets in policing have disappeared since the Home Secretary's pronouncement in 2010, there is evidence that these and other targets remained. Rather than staying at strategic level, targets sank instead to sub-force level (i.e. with managers at a lower level), changing little of policing practice (Curtis, 2015). In the current climate, with the accent on public protection, terrorism and neighbourhood policing, Neyroud (2008) rightly suggests that more sophisticated measurements of organisational success are required. The FBI were recently criticised for publishing figures relating to terrorist activity disrupted by the agency. Seemingly to demonstrate their success in the fight against terrorism in the USA, the FBI were unable (or unwilling) to qualify what they meant by disruption or to provide evidence of their successes.

Since the Home Office Circular in 1993, and the 2001 Government White Paper, criteria for measuring organisational success have been redefined a number of times. The National Policing Plan (2004–8) made it clear that forces would be assessed on a variety of areas, not merely crime detection rates. By utilising the Policing Performance Assessment Framework (PPAF), forces were assessed on key areas such as user satisfaction, citizen focus, public confidence, performance in fairness and diversity, crime levels (taken from national statistics), offences brought to justice, sanctioned detections, domestic violence, traffic, quality of life of members of the public, frontline policing, and use of resources. These criteria were set through 'best value' legislation and were capable of being changed annually. The framework attempted to compare forces that were geographically and socially similar in order to compare 'like for like'. Even this framework fell into disrepute because of doubts relating to the comparisons that were being made (Tong, 2005). Were they really comparing like for like when each police service might have different policing needs and priorities based on their unique make-up? 'Sanction detections' included where a suspect had been charged, cautioned, reprimanded, given a final warning or had offences taken into consideration (TIC). 'Non-sanction' detections included where a victim or witness was unable or unwilling to give testimony, where a case was not in the public interest to proceed or the offender was *doli incapax* (under the age of criminal responsibility). 'Brought to justice' (BTJ) criteria included where a suspect had been convicted at court, cautioned, reprimanded, etc., as well as having taken offences into consideration at court. It can be seen that the issue of convictions has been included, although these are discussed in the context of police performance, not individual investigators or investigations. Neyroud (2008) suggests that the brought-to-justice criteria were often utilised to measure the criminal justice system as a whole rather than policing on its own, bearing in mind convictions can fail outside of the influence of the police (i.e. failure within other agencies; see Kirby, 2013).

The PEEL review, an ongoing process of reviewing police effectiveness, is carried out by HMIC annually. The latest report on police effectiveness (HMIC, 2017) assesses the police in relation to criteria such as prevention of crime and anti-social behaviour, investigation of crime, catching and managing offenders, protection of the vulnerable, and effectiveness in relation to serious and organised crime. All of this under the headline of public safety and crime prevention (we have discussed some of the report's findings in Chapter 2). While this process does demonstrate a move away from detection figures as the sole measure of success, towards a more sophisticated approach, detections are still central to considerations. When assessing investigative performance, detections are a natural outcome of the process and easier to measure (Newburn and Reiner, 2004). Curtis (2015) recently encouraged police leadership to ensure that all performance measures link to the forces purpose and Police and Crime plan. Forces were encouraged to reconsider targets that relate to recorded crime, response times and call-handling. Utilising purely quantitative measures such as detections to assess the success or otherwise of individual investigations and individual investigators has been criticised for many reasons, which will be discussed shortly. The *outcome* focus will also be considered in the context of individual performance. In addition, the *process* of investigation as a measure or potential measure of success will receive critical attention.

Measuring individual performance and success within investigations

We have seen how clearance rates alone are generally unreliable as a measure of investigative effectiveness, as figures can easily be manipulated (Greenberg et al, 1972; Greenwood, 1970; Greenwood et al, 1977; Skolnick, 1966). Moreover, Greenwood et al (1977) found that arrest and clearance rates varied according to many issues other than just investigative training, staffing, procedures and organisation. Rather, the rates were determined by size of department, regional variations and workload. According to the RAND study (1977), variations in clearance rates could be explained by the unique characteristics of each area, not merely by organisation and deployment of investigators.

Cohen and Chaiken (1987) conducted research in the USA to try to discover the best means of selecting investigators and evaluating their performance. The main focus of their research was to identify individuals working as 'uniformed response' who would be more likely to be successful as detectives. The research did not suggest means of measuring the success of individual detectives, but the principles can be utilised for that purpose. Cohen and Chaiken (1987) undertook a thorough review of the research literature as well as conducting interviews with many different police departments. From the relevant literature, they identified that written civil service examinations were the best predictors of investigative success. These tests measured cognitive ability linked to specific areas such as intelligence and abstract reasoning. The study went on to discuss other potential predictors of investigative success; for instance, in relation to arrests.

According to Cohen and Chaiken (1987), simply determining the quantity of arrests was not sufficient. They identified *quality* of arrests as indicative of success in contrast to quantity. Quantity of arrests alone did not give an indication of an officer's discerning behaviour in identifying the successful cases, whereas quality of arrests did. Successful cases in the context of quality of arrests concerned cases that led eventually to prosecutions. This was an interesting perspective, bearing in mind most studies of investigative work research the investigative process up until arrest but rarely beyond that (Brodeur, 2010; see also Eck, 1983) Cohen and Chaiken (1987) also identified other factors that could potentially predict good investigator performance. These factors included demonstrable and proven ability in the field, daily work behaviours (such as absenteeism, complaints and awards), qualifications (such as education and experience) and finally a set of subjective traits that could be identified by a supervisory appraisal system (such as motivation, stability and persistence). Interestingly, these subjective traits have been identified as important in studies in the UK and beyond (O'Neill, 2011; Westera et al, 2014).

Other studies have explored alternative ways of measuring success within criminal investigations. Forst et al (1977) suggested that *quality* of arrests was more significant for predicting future successful detective candidates. Forst et al (1977) analysed data from several different police agencies and suggested that arrest convictability was a better determinant for assessing police performance rather than just simple arrest figures. He suggested two productivity measures: the number of convictions and conviction rate (the number of convictions denotes the number of convictions an investigator has obtained, regardless of the number of arrests they have made). In Forst's view, this could be a more accurate measure of investigator productivity than arrests. He considered that the conviction rate (dividing the total number of arrests ending in conviction by the total number of arrests) was a more appropriate measure because it distinguished an officer's discerning behaviour in not making unwarranted arrests. The disadvantage of Forst's proposed measure was that it was devised primarily as a tool to distinguish patrol officers likely to make good detectives. Forst accepted this limitation but did insist that this was a useful measure in two respects. First, he suggested it had its uses for selecting patrol officers to go on to become detectives. Second, he suggested that it was a useful tool for promoting detectives.

Even assuming that Forst's proposal could transpose to the UK, it is somewhat dated, and modern policing may not work in the same way. Modern volume crime investigation, managed as it is by crime management systems and processes mean that investigators do not arrest suspects as often as they once did. For instance, some volume crime departments have investigators purely dealing with persons who have already been arrested. Some investigators may spend their time interviewing suspects and not dealing with the consequent charge and file completion. All these issues need to be taken into account when trying to assess investigative success. Despite the disadvantages mentioned, the main advantage of using Forst's measure was that it was designed to measure the performance of individual investigators, although again it was based on quantitative measures relating to output. A final disadvantage is that commentators are agreed that the conviction of an offender at trial is reliant on many factors out of the control of the investigator, so to measure their success or otherwise at this point is inappropriate (Kirby, 2013).

Eck (1983) devised a formula for numerically scoring investigations based on the level of difficulty of cases. If, for instance, a case had very limited information at the time of its allocation to an investigator, it would be given a relatively low difficulty score (The score given would depend on the probability of solving the crime with such limited information). Each investigator's workload would need to be scrutinised over a period of time and an 'expected solvability level' calculated for each individual (based on the average difficulty score of cases allocated). For instance, an investigator might receive a solvability level of three for ten assigned cases. He or she would be expected to solve at least three of these allocated cases. An investigator solving three is performing to expected levels, an investigator solving one is performing below expected levels, while an investigator solving more than three is operating above expectations. Once again, the weakness of this approach to modern investigations in EW is that the hard-to-solve volume crime cases are invariably screened out of the system.

Maguire et al (1992) were commissioned by the Home Office to identify alternatives to the 'clear-up rate' as a standard measure of investigative effectiveness in the UK. They found much grassroots dissatisfaction with the measure. Instead, detectives favoured alternative measures such as peer assessment and victim and public surveys. Overwhelmingly, they favoured line manager appraisal. Some respondents commented that this was because their line manager was the person who 'knew them best'. Within the study, Maguire et al (1992) also considered other potential means of assessing investigative performance. Similar to Eck (1983), they suggested a distinction between 'high detectability' offences and 'low detectability' offences. High detectability offences were those crimes reported to the police where there was already a named suspect or good leads available. In these types of cases, the probability of a successful outcome was increased because it was more readily solvable. Low detectability offences encompassed investigations where at the time of report there were no obvious leads or offenders (this is not dissimilar to 'self-solvers' and 'whodunits' identified in homicide investigations by Innes, 2003). By analysing cases in these two categories, Maguire et al (1992) were able to compare investigative success across different police areas (their gathering of the data was resource-intensive, as they had to analyse each separate case from the beginning to ascertain whether it was a low detectability or high detectability case). They found that a large proportion of low detectability cases were made up of volume crime offences such as burglary, theft of pedal cycle, theft from motor vehicle, theft of motor vehicle and other theft. When they compared success across areas they found that differences could be explained by a complex set of factors such as the type of community policed, the crime mix (in terms of the prevalence of high and low detectability offences), relationship between CID and the uniform branch, specific local practices (i.e. proactive work, focus on particular offending) and crime screening practices. Many of these factors would be outside the control of individual investigators. Indeed, as Kirby (2013) posits, factors such as the quality of liaison with other agencies, witness and victim evidence not coming up to proof at court, decisions by the CPS, and decisions at court by officials and juries are often factors outside the control of individual investigators. Therefore, it is difficult to judge investigators based on issues that are largely outside their sphere of influence.

The issue of low detectability offences being used as a measure of success is likely to be fruitless in the modern era. Due to crime management policies and practices, forces screen crimes before cases are allocated to investigators. Cases where there are few leads are screened out and are never investigated (ACPO, 2001; Burrows et al, 2005). They are merely recorded, routine questions are asked, and they are then filed unless and until further information or evidence comes to light (ACPO, 2001). In fact, a recent small-scale study found that in austerity, screening *out* volume crime is a practice that might expand (James and Mills, 2012). It is clear that due to structural and procedural changes brought about by the sheer volume of reported crime, low detectability offences are routinely filed and investigators receive high detectability offences to investigate (an interesting notion that merits further attention). This situation will not be reflected in serious, complex and major crimes however, as there is no screening process other than the serious nature of the crime itself.

In his research on homicide detectives in the UK, Innes (2003) noted how, traditionally, detectives (unlike their uniformed counterparts) had been expected to produce results (in terms of detections). He cites the tension between wanting to catch hard-core criminals and the need to continue to gain a 'decent' number of detections. Unfortunately, such tension can lead to exactly the kind of detection-driven culture that can cultivate corrupt practices (Walker, 1992; Reiner, 1998; Patrick, 2011a; Patrick, 2011b) and MOJ (Savage and Milne, 2007). Innes is not just talking about homicide investigators here, because the pressure for 'volume' detection figures is probably less in major crime departments than it is in general crime investigation offices. The foregoing points to the need for a more sophisticated measure of investigative effectiveness.

The use of purely outcome measures to identify effectiveness, whether on an organisational or individual level, is extremely problematic (Tong, 2005). First, such a focus may lead investigators to chase detections and deal with cases thought to require the minimum of effort in order to achieve the desired outcome. In this sense, all of the high ideals of professional practice are potentially sacrificed in order to achieve detections (Maguire and Norris, 1994). Important parts of the investigative process may be ignored, with investigators cutting corners in an effort to get a result. Culturally the chase for quantitative figures potentially leads not only to unprofessional practice but also to corrupt practices (Reiner, 1998; Walker, 1992). As Maguire et al.

(1992) identified, the drive for performance in the form of quantity of detections can take precedence over investigative quality. Second, measuring investigative performance by detections alone fails to address the variety of investigations in which investigators become involved that do not have a positive disposal outcome. These will be dealt with in more detail later, but an example will suffice at this point.

An officer may be allocated a volume crime to investigate. They may spend valuable time investigating, but soon uncover evidence that suggests that the victim's account is false. The victim is challenged, and they admit that they made up the allegation in order to claim on their insurance. The investigating officer will be able to reclassify the crime as 'no crime'. In this sense, the investigation has been successful inasmuch as it has identified the truth and deleted a false crime statistic from the records. However, this does not materialise as a positive disposal on the record of the investigator (Of course, another crime can now be raised that is detected-the fraud perpetrated in order to make a false insurance claim, but this doesn't reflect the work done to ensure a false crime is removed from the record). In this sense detection figures do not provide the whole picture. Third, quantitative measures alone fail to measure the contribution of highly motivated, competent and productive officers who are regularly called on to assist colleagues without adding to their own detection figures. In other situations, investigators may be called on to attend incidents to consider whether a criminal offence has been committed (a classic situation envisaged by CPIA as constituting a criminal investigation). They will spend time conducting enquiries (for instance at the scene of a sudden death) to try to discover what has happened. Through investigative effort, they may be able to piece together the last few hours of a person's life to help understand why and how they died. In a large percentage of cases there will be a determination that this is not a criminal matter but a report may be required for the coroner. This type of thorough investigation does not add to the crime statistics in these situations described. However, they do contribute to the system of coronial investigation of death, and a thorough investigation will assist the final determination of cause. Any notion of investigative success should be able to encompass the range of investigations undertaken including those not strictly bearing on criminal justice outcomes.

This discussion raises further questions in relation to individual investigative effectiveness. Should *some* measures be in place to ensure investigator accountability? Would it further erode public confidence if there were *no* means of measuring individual effectiveness? Does the taxpayer have a right to know that there are measures in place to ensure that investigators are doing the job they are expected to do, and that they are doing it well? In order to discover the thoughts of modern investigators, officers (213) in six different police forces within EW were asked to take answer a questionnaire (O'Neill, 2011). One metropolitan force was represented, one northern force, one force from the midlands, one from the south east of England, one from the south west of England, and one from Wales. This was to ensure that the six forces were representative of forces in EW. Questionnaires were distributed to officers from constable (both PC and DC), up to Detective Chief Inspector. No questionnaires were returned when left at stations or sent through the post. This response rate may have been low due to officer workload and time needed for the study. While each force generously stated it would allow officers to fill in the questionnaires in duty time, many insisted that due to heavy workload this was impractical, and in some cases, impossible. The nature of volume crime investigations is that planned events often have to come second to responding to new incidents, arrests and situations. It is noteworthy that officers blamed heavy workload when austerity had not yet cut budgets a further 20%. Sixty-four (64) officers agreed to take part in the study, some opting to fill in the questionnaire themselves, others because of work commitments preferring to answer questions as they were asked by the researcher. The response rate was 30.5%. The data was analysed utilising both statistical analysis of the quantitative data (using statistical package SPSS) and content analysis of answers to open questions. The qualitative responses yielded some further quantitative data.

Respondents were asked what in their opinion amounted to success in volume crime investigation. This was an open question designed to gain rich data, uninfluenced by previous research or the researcher. Content analysis was conducted on the subsequent responses. The different responses were classified, counted and identified into most recurring themes. Victim satisfaction was most frequently mentioned, while conviction, detections and thoroughness ranked second, third and fourth respectively. Getting to the truth ranked joint fifth with justice. Arresting/identifying an offender ranked joint seventh with ensuring all leads were pursued. Good case papers ranked ninth (O'Neill and Milne, 2014). Interestingly, these themes represent a mixture of areas that can be achieved by individual effort (for instance arrest, thoroughness, and good case papers) interspersed with areas that an individual alone is less likely to be able to control (for instance convictions, victim satisfaction, or justice). It was interesting that volume crime investigators looked beyond detection criteria to issues such as victim satisfaction and conviction (see Brookman and Innes,

2013, discussed later in this chapter). This was not the same however, when they were asked to identify how individual investigative success could be measured.

When asked whether they felt it was possible to measure the success of investigative work. 43 (66%) indicated 'yes', 17 (26%) indicated 'no', while 5 (8%) indicated *both* 'yes' and 'no'. Those answering this question were then asked to elaborate, and to detail what they felt the best measures were. All of those who indicated 'yes' to the question identified a number of different measures that should and could be used to measure investigative success (O'Neill and Milne, 2014). Detections were ranked first, convictions second, victim satisfaction third and thoroughness fourth. Respondents were also asked what they felt the best ways to measure the success of an individual *investigator* were. Detections ranked first, while convictions, victim satisfaction and tutor or supervisor assessment ranked second, third and fourth respectively.

Respondents were then asked what they felt the best ways to measure the success of an individual *investigation* were. Detection again ranked first, thoroughness ranked second, convictions ranked third and victim satisfaction fourth. Supervisor assessment ranked only sixth. Responses revealed that detections were identified most frequently when considering the most appropriate ways to measure success of either individual investigations or individual investigators. Respondents choosing this method of measurement appeared to be sceptical of its reliability if used in isolation, and felt that in reality this was a fairly crude and unreliable measure. Many respondents were clear that they felt that detections alone did not provide the whole picture relating to investigative success. This can be seen in some of the following responses.

Of the respondents who answered the question around how best to measure success, over 50% identified more than detections rates alone as being the most appropriate method to use. Respondents answering 'yes' to the question of whether it was possible to measure success were asked to identify in what ways it was possible to measure it. Some of the qualitative responses were:

> 'Detections, convictions, cases disproved/no crimed, and witness satisfaction....However, not by statistics alone. Each investigation would have to be marked or graded by an independent reviewer who reviewed the investigation, not the end result.'

'Quantity is easier to measure than gathering quality as you can see how many crimes/prisoners a person has dealt with and compare against their peers. But this does not always reflect the effort and time that may have been put in by another or on a particular job.'

And finally:

'The only way to measure this would be for the investigations to be read through. Success should not be measured on detected rate alone as this paints a false picture. You could have one officer dealing with very simple investigations with a high-detected rate and an officer dealing with more complex, serious jobs with a lower detected figure. Both working equally hard and well but the nature of the investigation must always be considered.'

For those people who indicated that they felt it was not possible to measure investigative success, some of the explanations were:

'One case may be successful in a way you can't monitor in terms of performance......You can't detect an undetectable crime.'

'Success usually is seen as number of detections achieved which does not always reflect reality of investigations carried out.'

'An £88,000 robbery is exactly the same performance indicator as a schoolboy who has been robbed of his phone.'

Investigators were asked a number of questions relating to success and how it should be measured in relation to both individual investigators and individual investigations. Detections ranked highest in answer to all of these questions. However, respondents invariably felt that the clear up rates alone should not be used as the sole indicator of success, but should be among a number of different criteria. Common areas of measurement cited were conviction rates, victim satisfaction and thoroughness.

In a second study, officers were asked to nominate successful investigators from among their peers. They all listed a top five. Ranking lists were provided for each of the six crime groups, using this subjective criteria. Officers were ranked depending on the number of nominations they received from peers. In a third study, the study intended to use objective criteria to rank the investigators. However, problems arose. Participating forces were asked to provide data in the form of number of crimes that each investigator had dealt with over a two-and-a-half-year period together with detection rate, arrests, case files submitted, convictions and solvability factors. No single police force was able to provide all of the data requested. There was a disparity in relation to computer systems used by different forces. Not all of the forces, for example, had linked data systems in their area, where all of these criteria were capable of being searched. Obtaining the requested data would have required consulting a number of databases within each force. As the only consistently recorded outcome was crime detections this tends to support the contention of Chatterton (2008) that the system of performance measurement means that conviction is not a concern to police senior management, and is therefore not measured. Previous research had identified the difficulty of finding some of the information sought in this study (Burrows et al, 2005). Tilly et al (2007, p 241) later stated: 'The paper trail from the investigative process involves many components and can – even for volume crime cases that are undetected be substantial.'

Because of these findings, the study concentrated on detections, as this was the only consistent data available. A ranking list was compiled from the detection figures over a 30-month period. The top five and bottom five were identified, five from within each of the participating volume crime teams. These officers were then subjected to tests in areas considered by modern investigators to relate to successful investigators. These emerged from the first study. Respondents identified personality, critical thinking, empathy and intelligence (O'Neill, 2011). No significant differences were found between the high and low sets. This could mean that there is little difference between modern investigators in relation to the facets identified, and that other factors distinguish successful performers, or it could point to weakness in the criteria of success used to distinguish the high and low sets. Fahsing and Ask (2017) suggest the objective measures used are unreliable because of their inherent unreliability.

Some respondents highlighted, the need to look at victim satisfaction as a potential measure of success. This area of measurement is relatively new in policing circles and only became prevalent as a measure relatively recently. Victim satisfaction surveys have become fashionable; however, they rarely deal with the success or otherwise of an individual officer but deal predominantly with a victim's interaction with the police service. Some studies have shown that professionalism of investigators had an impact on victim satisfaction (Brandl and Horvath, 1991). Professionalism was broken down into four elements: Courteousness, understanding, concern and competence. Interestingly, victim satisfaction was impacted by investigative effort in property crimes but not as much in personal crimes. A further study in the UK linked victim satisfaction to thoroughness of investigation in crimes such as burglary and auto crime (Gill et al, 1996). Of course, victim satisfaction in specific cases is different from other actors satisfaction in a case (i.e. a witness), and is to be distinguished from citizen satisfaction on a more general level. Often the police may undertake investigative strategies even though such strategies may yield little, for the purpose of victim satisfaction and reassurance (Gill et al, 1996). Investigators in the O'Neill (2011) study felt that victim satisfaction was inherently problematic. If a victim is satisfied with police response in a crime, because someone has been brought to justice for their crime, who is credited with the success? The police in general? An arresting officer? The investigator who completes the investigation and becomes the OIC? On a final note, the IPCC has suggested (IPCC, 2013a) that victim care should be at the heart of performance measures, and this is particularly important in areas such as sexual offences and violent crime. This reflects somewhat the conclusions of the Stern review (Stern, 2010) which stated that success in rape investigations should be measured in terms of support and care for victims, rather than detections. The IPCC made their observation against the backdrop of an investigation into the MPS Sapphire Team at Southwark, which had been accused of placing gaming practices and crime statistics above victim care.

Gorby (2013) considered the measurement of police performance in the context of the role of uniformed officers. From the starting point that the police only deal with crime matters for around 25% of the time (Carr et al, 1980), he suggested that traditional measures of police performance failed to incorporate behavioural elements such as how they interacted with citizens, courtesy, friendliness, their ability to communicate, their ability to de-escalate confrontational situations, and their ability to make independent decisions. Gorby suggested that measuring these facets would provide a more useful measure of effective performance in order to improve the behaviour of officers. This supports in some way the consideration of Bayley and Bittner (1984) who identified a range of possible outcomes of a police interaction with citizens, many of which do not involve a measurable outcome in the sense of an arrest or a crime detection (this has been discussed in Chapter 5).

Brookman and Innes (2013) conducted qualitative studies with senior detectives engaged in homicide investigations. Interviews were primarily by way of semi-structured interviews with officers from the rank of inspector through to the rank of chief superintendent. The authors spent time on fieldwork, observing the detectives conducting 20 homicide investigations and seven further major crime investigations (nearly 50 hours' total observations). Moreover, they attended briefings, had informal interviews with practitioners, and observed the work of the homicide detectives working in Major Incident rooms. They also linked to a further study they had undertaken for the Home Office in relation to the use of Community Impact Assessments (CIA). That study was conducted between 2004 and 2008 and involved semi-structured interviews with the public following high-profile murders within the community. Much of the second study informed Innes's work on the effect of signal crimes on the community (Innes, 2004, 2014). Brookman and Innes (2013) found that modern homicide investigators had a much more nuanced concept of success than one might expect if they had just read the literature on past detective indiscretions. Rather than being wedded to the notion of 'locking up the bad guys', the detectives revealed that there were added dimensions to their thinking. These primarily related to four distinct areas.

First, some detectives espoused the classic outcome mode of thinking in terms of seeing the identification, charge and prosecution of 'the bad guys' as a key determinant of success. The interesting perspective here was the suggestion that detectives saw success as more than just 'detection' of a crime. Crime detections in the UK are still judged on the outcome measures of criminal justice disposals (i.e. charges, summonses, cautions or reprimands). The issue of conviction at court is not measured. It is interesting to see that detectives in homicide cases saw the eventual conviction as crucial. They saw it as important that the sentence reflected the seriousness of the crime, and that the case could withstand legal and judicial scrutiny with regards to the processes and procedures used by them. Thus, in major crime, the detectives sense of success went beyond detection criteria (even though they accepted that much of what happens in court is beyond their control once it gets there). An interesting question would be whether investigators perceptions are linked to the seriousness of the offence. Do they have the same views in volume crime offences or serious and complex crime offences? Particularly when the crime is ostensibly detected once a criminal justice outcome is applied.

Second, success was seen by some respondents as more procedural, indicating that it could be measured in terms of the perceived quality of the investigation rather than its outcome. Completing an investigation that had demonstrably complied with procedural requirements was considered to be important. As Brookman and Innes note, some cases, while able to demonstrate a good outcome, could not demonstrate a good procedure. Sometimes this would reflect later criticism of the investigation but not jeopardise a conviction (i.e. the Soham Investigation and subsequent criticism from the Bichard Report, 2004), while seemingly sound investigations might later be determined to have been so procedurally and legally fraught that they directly impact on the propriety of the original conviction (i.e. several miscarriage of justice cases; for instance, the Birmingham Six and the Guildford Four). Brookman and Innes (2013) note: 'The requirements of criminal law and criminal procedure (that) are embedded in police constructions of successful investigations' (Brookman and Innes, 2013, p 297), suggesting subtle shifts from the view that a conviction is all. Third, success can be viewed in terms of how the investigation serves to reassure the public, and fourth, in terms of how use is made of the learning from the case to help inform prevention strategies for the future. A final point that is raised in this discussion of success within homicide investigations is the nature of the team and whether it is possible to measure individual success by case outcome where a team ethos exists. As an example, we have seen how a large number of people form a team in homicide investigations. One SIO may lead, but many will actively work on an investigation. How can the team be measured against a conviction, or lack of one? Should they be measured on such a crude outcome or do more subtle and sophisticated measures need to be undertaken in relation to the processes they undertake and the quality of those outcomes (i.e. a specialist interviewer and the outcome of a good interview)? In addition, there is a proliferation of departments all dealing with distinct areas of investigative practice. For instance, how does one measure the success or otherwise of a public protection unit, or specialist team investigating online child exploitation or a safeguarding team? The discussion here leads inexorably to the conclusion that effective supervisor and managerial appraisals should play an important role in ensuring professional practice, although its ineffectiveness and subjectivity in relation to detectives has been the subject of criticism in the past (Maguire and Norris, 1992).

Conclusion

What constitutes success in criminal investigations is an issue that has taxed researchers, police practitioners and politicians for some time. When viewed from an organisational perspective, the idea of success is often subsumed within the prevailing aims of the current political stance, and thought of in this way is a flexible concept difficult to identify. What amounts to success in one paradigm may not be success in another. The former reliance on detection figures has been complemented with concerns around victim care, risk management, public protection, and elements of professional practice. Moreover, the difficulty of defining success can be multi-faceted, depending on the stance, affiliations or role of the individual judging it. On an individual level, detectives of the past gained status through locking up criminals and in this sense, success was viewed entirely through the lens of charge or convictions. Such a focus has often served to incentivise misconduct in order to secure convictions, yet the prevailing culture of detectives still viewed it as the core narrative of detective work. Pragmatism has also given way to such naïve notions of success. Research has indicated that investigations are rarely solved by detective brilliance, and that cases are generally solved through the assistance of the public and uniformed patrol officers who admittedly have a 24/7 presence. Teamwork is often key in modern investigations, as they tend to rely on the input of a range of individuals performing different functions. This leads directly to the difficulty of investigative success as it relates to victim satisfaction. Because of the foregoing, it is likely that victim satisfaction is going to be rare. Where victims are dissatisfied with an investigation, the source of that dissatisfaction may not be the person designated as the lead investigator for that crime. Analysis of the dissatisfaction might reveal that what went wrong was out of the influence of the lead investigator. Moreover, where a victim is satisfied with the police investigation, there are a multiplicity of reasons why that might be the case, many of which may not have been influenced by the lead investigator at all. Consider the example already discussed of the burglar caught in the act and passed to a detective officer to investigate the crime. If convicted, the victim might be very satisfied with the police response, they may even be led to send a letter of appreciation for the work of the detective. Yet the constable catching the criminal in the act of committing the crime was a significant factor in its detection. Analysis of purely quantitative figures fails to ascertain the nuanced picture. This would also be true where a person is caught by fingerprints or DNA. Whose good work will the victim be satisfied with? The historical accent on arrest rates and arrest convictability rates (Forst et al, 1977) do not appear to work well with the modern era. As can be seen from the make-up of some of the participating crime groups, many investigators react to the crimes that they are given to investigate. In a large majority of cases, many deal with prisoners already arrested by their operational peers. Many of the cases given to officers to investigate now relate to high-detectability crimes. Many low-detectability volume crimes are filed at source because they fail the relevant screening criteria that determine whether investigative resources should be directed at them. But surely some measures must be in place in the modern era to assess the effectiveness of individual investigators and their investigations? It appears that reliance is placed on active supervision and management, and the PIP process to ensure that standards are met.

Further reading

Brookman, F. and Innes, M. (2013) 'The problem of success. What is a good homicide investigation?' *Policing and Society*, 23(3): 292–310.

Neyroud, P. (2008) 'Past, Present and Future Performance: Lessons and Prospects for the Measurement of Police Performance'. *Policing*, 2(3): 340–8.

SEVEN

IPCC reports on investigations

Introduction

Effective oversight is essential for police legitimacy and accountability. The IPCC plays an important oversight function. Whether their functions, powers, remit and effectiveness are sufficient is open to debate (Home Affairs Committee, 2013; Smith, 2009). However, theory would suggest that they oversee the disciplinary process across EW and, once cases are referred to them, they can choose to independently investigate, manage or supervise what they deem to be the most serious of cases (National Audit Office, 2008). Investigations conducted by one of several commissioners are considered to be the most independent investigations, overseen by a commissioner who by law cannot have a policing background. The IPCC investigate cases and make recommendations in relation to individual culpability or organisational learning on the part of the police. Waddington (2015) suggests that the idea of the police 'learning lessons' is hollow rhetoric because time and again the same themes emerge from cases, with little evidence of real learning (Waddington, 2015). He posits that police responses are specific to the situation rather than to underlying, systemic causes. Support for this contention comes from Dame Anne Owers, who remarked recently that often forces view an officer's dismissal as the solution to a problem when it may not be (NPCC, 2016). This chapter reports an examination of published IPCC reports from two periods (2004–9 and 2010–15). The research aim was to compare criminal investigation failings within the two periods. IPCC recommendations were considered from individual and organisational perspectives. This chapter attempts to test the accuracy of Waddington's assertion that lessons are not being learnt, despite contrary assurances from the police. The role of the IPCC will be discussed, as will the areas of learning that result from published reports and their recommendations.

The IPCC

The IPCC was created by the Police Reform Act 2002 amid suggestions that the former Police Complaints Authority (PCA) system was ineffective in holding police to account (Macpherson, 1999; Savage, 2013). The PCA could not conduct independent investigations, nor did it have the power or resources to carry out sufficient numbers of investigations. In fact, its scope was significantly limited (Harrison and Cunneen, 2000; Hardwick, 2006). This was highlighted most sharply in the Lawrence case, prompting Macpherson (1999) to recommend change (Savage, 2013). It was claimed that the new organisation would provide a watching function, have capacity to investigate the most serious cases independently and have oversight of the police disciplinary mechanism. In its first few years, it investigated a number of serious cases and seemingly lived up to its billing (Hardwick, 2006). However, questions have been raised around the organisations independence. How independent could it be if it answered to the Home Office, the same department overseeing the police? Moreover, the IPCC also lacked equivalent police powers to enable them to effectively investigate, and a percentage of their staff were from the very ranks of the service they were intended to investigate (Smith, 2009). In terms of citizen oversight of the police, while the IPCC fares favourably when compared to similar institutions around the world, the Police Ombudsman of Northern Ireland (PONI) is described as an exemplar of a system entirely independent of the police (Porter and Prenzler, 2012). The PONI investigate all disciplinary matters relating to the police (Porter and Prenzler, 2012). Additionally, the IPCC has been criticised for only conducting 1% of its cases independently, while the remaining 99% are conducted by the police with some supervision or oversight (Home Affairs Committee, 2013). Even the 1% of independent investigations require assistance from the police. Savage (2013) has also highlighted that independence on the part of IPCC investigators can often be diluted by empathic attitudes towards the police role, with IPCC staff not wishing to 'rock the boat' for fear of affecting ongoing relationships or being seen as too critical (Savage, 2013).

The function of the IPCC is underpinned by a set of values. These are independence, respect for human rights, justice, diversity, integrity and openness (IPCC, 2005; Hardwick, 2006). Part of the role of the IPCC, in addition to oversight of the disciplinary process and deciding on investigation levels, is to promote best practice within the police, allowing forces to learn lessons from the most serious of failings. Since 2014, Chief Officers have a statutory obligation to respond to recommendations made by the IPCC, although the IPCC do not have power to inspect forces for compliance (Anti-social Behaviour, Crime and Policing Act, 2014). A concordat drawn up between CoP,

HMIC and the IPCC in 2014 does ensure, though, that HMIC are aware of IPCC findings and they have the opportunity to inspect forces under their statutory responsibilities (CoP/HMIC/IPCC, 2014). They undertake research in problematic areas (i.e. custody deaths), while also publishing a bulletin for forces entitled *Learning the lessons*. This is intended to distil learning from IPCC cases and act as an informative vehicle to assist police improvement (IPCC, 2005; National Audit Office, 2008). Since the first issue in 2007, this has been well received, with a large percentage of police respondents feeling that the publication has been both useful and relevant to their role (National Audit Office, 2008; IPCC, 2017). What is less well understood is whether the police organisation: a) really learns from those lessons; b) changes policy and practice as a result of previous cases; c) ensures that mechanisms are in place to check that policy and practice has changed; d) ensures that individual staff members are aware of and understand any changes adopted. Is publication of the material sufficient to embed new systems and processes? The matter is complicated by the fact that police forces are distinct entities tied to local policies and procedures, despite there being a complex system of national protocols.

Dame Anne Owers (IPCC Chair), noted some resistance to deeper learning opportunities as a result of IPCC recommendations (NPCC, 2016). Such resistance can come from a distrust of an organisation which, from the practitioner point of view, becomes the adversary whenever high-profile cases go wrong. There is ongoing discussion in relation to how a learning ethos can replace a discipline ethos to enable the police service to become a learning organisation. Distrust of the nature of IPCC investigations, the competence of the organisation's investigators with little investigative experience, combined with evidence of incompetent handling of cases by the IPCC, do not engender a spirit of cooperation to achieve learning for the future. In order to identify whether there were recurring themes in police failings, and to consider Waddington's claim, this study sought to examine IPCC published investigation reports that touched on criminal investigation.

Method

In July 2015 a Freedom of Information request was sent to the IPCC, requesting a list of published IPCC investigation reports since 2005. A list containing 220 entries was returned; however, some entries concerned the same case. After multiple references had been eliminated from the sample, retaining IPCC reports into different aspects of the same investigation, 200 cases were left. The response generated by the IPCC highlighted the existence of an IPCC archive containing investigation reports from the period since 2010. This contained 358 cases. The two databases were cross-referred and a total of 362 separate cases were identified.

All 362 case references were reviewed to identify those with links to criminal investigation. A number of cases referenced (108) were not accompanied by case reports or links to case reports, and were eliminated from the sample. A total of 254 cases were analysed in more detail to extract the following information: date of occurrence; date of report; type of case; names of civilians involved; type of investigation; number of officers involved; individual and organisational recommendations made. Cases such as deaths in custody, police shootings and internal corruption investigations were eliminated, unless relevant to the process of criminal investigation. Only cases that identified specific organisational or individual failings within criminal investigations were retained. Cases investigated but not substantiated by the IPCC were also eliminated. Cases were divided between the period 2004–9, and 2010–15, based on the dates they were published rather than when they occurred. The justification for this course of action was to consider cases' potential for influencing police learning. While police forces will have been aware of the incidents under investigation, and may even have carried out their own internal investigations, the publication dates of the IPCC reports represent a key starting point from which improvements (if any) in police performance can be examined. In total, 62 cases were retained, 21 from the first time period, 41 from the second time period. A thematic analysis was undertaken. Each case was analysed in more detail, codes were identified for emerging themes within the data, and comparison was made between the two six-year periods.

Findings

The 21 cases remaining in the 2004–9 time period contained 17 independent and four managed investigations. In total, 17 police forces were subject to investigation, with South Wales investigated the most frequently (four times) The MPS, Wiltshire and Essex were investigated twice each, with the remaining 13 (including BTP) investigated once. To clarify, this does not reflect the total number of times that forces within the sample were investigated by the IPCC, but represents published reports relevant to criminal investigation. Of the 21 cases, five (23%) related to DA investigations, four (19%) to rape investigations, three (14%) to death investigations (where police respond to a sudden or unexpected death), two (9%) related to child abuse, two (9%) related to missing persons, two (9%) concerned abduction, and the remainder related to crimes such as murder, GBH or threats to kill.

The 41 cases in the 2010–15 time period were represented by 40 independent investigations and one managed investigation. In total, 19 police forces were subject to investigation, with forces such as MPS (six times), Nottinghamshire (six times), Greater Manchester (six times), West Yorkshire (four times), South Wales (four times), and Essex (three times) being investigated the most. The types of cases in the second sample were represented most by DA cases: 16 (nearly 40%) of the cases were DA-related, four (10%) concerned rape investigations, four (10%) were homicide investigations, two (5%) historical sexual abuse investigations, two (5%) anti-social behaviour reports, and two (5%) death investigations. The remaining cases were robbery, theft, GBH, criminal damage and burglary investigations. The higher number of cases in the second period does not necessarily indicate a growth in the number of cases failing. The number of cases investigated by the IPCC has risen steadily since its inception in 2004 as their resources and expertise in investigations has risen (IPCC, 2016). That said, there was a rise in the percentage of cases relating to DA (23% in the first period, 40% in the second period). Many of the reports concerning death concluded with a statement that there was no guarantee that the deceased victim would have been saved, even if the police had conducted their investigations thoroughly.

Individual failings (2004 to 2009)

In total, the IPCC made 57 recommendations concerning officers and staff in the 21 cases. They recommended that two officers should be subject to gross misconduct proceedings, 26 officers and staff should be subject to misconduct proceedings, ten receive a written warning, eight receive words of advice, six receive advice or guidance, and a further three receive either extra training or explain to a victim why there was a delay in responding to their requests for information. In two cases, the IPCC felt there was misconduct on the part of officers, but they had since left the police service and could not be subject to disciplinary proceedings. Table 7.1 provides a breakdown of the key failings identified in the earlier time period.

Table 7.1: Key individual failings in IPCC reports, 2004–9

Individual failings	Number of examples
1. Poor investigation/lack of thoroughness	22
2. Failure to supervise or manage	16
3. Failure to recognise and deal with risk	8
4. Inadequate recording of rationale	7
5. No contemporaneous notes	3

Key themes emerging from this analysis were: over one third of the recommendations related to poor investigation or investigation depth (22 recommendations, 38%), over one quarter related to failings at supervisory or management level of criminal investigations (16 recommendations, 28%), failure to recognise and deal with risk (eight recommendations, 14%), and lack of recorded investigative rationale (seven recommendations, 12%) accounted for other main themes.

Individual failings (2010–15)

Within the 41 cases, the IPCC recommended that four officers should be subject to gross misconduct charges, 35 officers and staff should be subject to misconduct proceedings, 23 receive UPP, ten receive words of advice, ten receive advice or guidance, ten receive informal management action, three receive written warnings. and a further five receive either extra training, supervisory input or no further action. In 20 cases, the IPCC felt there was misconduct or gross misconduct on the part of officers, but they had since left the police service and could not be subject to disciplinary proceedings. In total, therefore, the IPCC suggested that 108 officers and staff in the 41 cases had conducted themselves in such a manner that required some form of intervention. Table 7.2 provides a breakdown of the failings.

Table 7.2: Key individual failings in IPCC reports, 2010–15

Individual failings	Number of examples
1. Poor investigation/lack of thoroughness	36
2. Failure to manage or supervise	20
3. Breach of law	19
4. Failure to recognise/deal with risk	11
5. Inadequate recording of rationale	5
6. No contemporaneous notes	4
7. Non-referral to social services	2

Key themes emerging were: poor investigation or investigation depth (36 recommendations, 29%), poor supervision or management of criminal investigations (20 recommendations, 17%), failure to recognise and deal with risk (11 recommendations, 10%), and lack of recorded rationale (five recommendations, 4.5%). While the category 'breach of law' appears significant here, 16 relate to two cases alleging deliberate breaches of law by officers in a single case, and three in another.

Failure to investigate or thoroughly investigate reports of crimes in both time periods included issues such as: failing to follow obvious and legitimate lines of inquiry; failing to secure evidence in a timely fashion; failure to secure scenes of crime; poor depth of statements; poor recording of contemporaneous notes from witnesses; making premature decisions about the identity of a perpetrator or concluding that a case did not require detailed investigation; failure to utilise new and existing legislation (such as the Protection from Harassment Act); failure to arrest in a timely fashion; failure to conduct sufficiently in depth interviews of suspects; and lack of compliance with disclosure law, policy and practice. In addition, there was evidence of a lack of compliance with existing policies and standard operating procedures. The failures to supervise or manage investigations stemmed from the original poor investigations undertaken by subordinates and ineffective close supervision or management to ensure that investigations were being carried out appropriately. Failure to recognise or deal with risk in the main related to DA cases, with the exception of failure to identify and manage risk in one threat-to-life case.

Organisational recommendations

In both time periods, there were more organisational recommendations than individual. In the earlier period, there were 131 organisational recommendations, eight of which were deemed national issues, and three relating to multi-agency protocols within investigations. In the later time period, there were 150 organisational recommendations, eight relating to national issues. The national issues between 2004 and 2009 primarily concerned recommendations on how forces should respond to honour-based violence. National recommendations between 2010 and 2015 related to call-handling issues, the use of domestic homicide reviews as per Home Office guidelines, and a change of legislation relating to life sentence offenders returning to the UK. Table 7.3 compares the main organisational themes from the two periods.

Table 7.3: Comparison of themes from organisational recommendations

Theme identified	2004–9 (131 recommendations)	2010–15 (150 recommendations)
Training required	18 (14%)	25 (17%)
Risk identification in DA cases	5 (4%)	12 (8%)
Lack of resources	6 (5%)	6 (4%)
Review policy	13 (10%)	5 (3%)
Reminder to staff/awareness	10 (8%)	10 (7%)
Call-handling issues	6 (5%)	13 (9%)

Percentages for the themes were recalculated on the basis of the number of times they occurred *per case,* and these are presented in Table 7.4 below:

Table 7.4: Theme percentages against case numbers

Theme identified	2004–9 (21 cases)	2010–15 (41 cases)
Training required	12 (57%)	25 (60%)
Risk identification in DA cases	5 (23%)	12 (29%)
Lack of resources	6 (28%)	6 (14%)
Review policy	13 (61%)	5 (12%)
Reminder to staff/awareness	10 (47%)	10 (24%)
Lack of experience	4(19%)	1(2%)
Call-handling issues	6 (28%)	13 (31%)

Between 2004 and 2009, 57% of the 21 cases contained recommendations relating to the need for more training for officers and staff. Between 2010 and 2015, this remained consistent, although slightly higher, at 60%. This demonstrates that a large number of published IPCC investigations have consistently recommended further training for officers and staff. While the number of recommendations relating to lack of resources remained consistent, there was a drop in the number of times this was referred to in individual cases. This was also the case where the IPCC recommended that forces should remind officers and staff of their need to comply with existing policy or standard procedures. Nearly half of cases in the earlier period made such recommendations (47%). However, in the later time period, nearly one quarter of reports identified the need to remind staff of existing policies or procedures (24%). In the earlier time period, lack of experience within the role was highlighted in 19% of cases, although in the later period this was only highlighted by the IPCC in one case. The number of cases where risk was a key factor rose from 23% in the earlier time period to 29% in the later time period. Almost all of these cases (apart from one) related to assessment of risk in DA cases. Call-handling issues appeared to have low percentages in both time periods (5% in the earlier period compared to 9% in the later period). However, when considered in relation to call-handling issues against case numbers, these occurred in 28% of the cases in the earlier time period and 31% of the cases in the later time period. Issues of lack of resources appeared to be more apparent in the earlier time period (28%, compared to 14% in the later period), Finally, there were a large proportion of cases in the earlier period where review of policy was recommended (61%) compared to the later period (12%).

Discussion

Poor Investigation

Within the individual recommendations, poor investigation and investigation depth remained a significant aspect of the cases (38% in the earlier time period compared to 29% in the later time period). Analysis of the failings suggests that many appear to be rudimentary enquiries an investigator would be expected to pursue were they to be undertaking a thorough investigation of the matter. Under the auspices of PIP, since 2005, investigators are trained at every level to investigate crime. All investigators have access to published guidance and policy relating to the process of investigation (for example, APP and MIM) yet these fundamental investigative failings appear to be consistent across both periods. Why do they still occur? Does it point to systemic failings in relation to the training and education of investigators, or some other possibility? While an FOI request relating to training identified little change in numbers in relation to those qualifying as PIP level two investigators, some research specifically mentions lack of training opportunities as a feature of modern policing. For example, the IPCC (2017) heard from frontline officers and police staff that formal training and development were largely absent for them. Unfortunately, it is not possible to discern how many staff felt this way. Lack of training or the inability of forces to conduct specialist training in austerity was considered to be a feature both pre- and post-austerity by police officers (Select Committee on Home Affairs, 2005; Chatterton, 2008; Hoggett et al, 2014). Moreover, James and Mills (2012) have questioned the positive rhetoric around PIP. Maguire and Norris (1994) suggested long ago that while training might be effective in pointing out previous failings, this is futile against the backdrop of the prevailing police culture. They suggested that if the underlying cultural values were not tackled, training was likely to be forgotten, with officers returning to 'business as usual' as soon as it was completed. A lack of face-to-face training, and the proliferation of e-learning packages and distance learning, while products of the modern era, are unlikely to make inroads into such mentality, particularly in areas such as DA (HMIC, 2014b), although this has not been subject to sufficient independent study.

Supervision and management

Poor management and supervision of investigations has been subject of comment in previous research on detective work from the early 1990s and beyond (Baldwin and Maloney, 1992: Maguire and Norris, 1992; Irving and Dunnighan, 1993). It has also been commented on in relation to police culture (Chan, 1996), officer stress (Shane, 2010), and supervision and management of investigations in a more modern context (Neyroud and Disley, 2007). This is another aspect of police investigation that is consistently identified as problematic, yet issues continue to arise. The PIP process was designed to ensure that specific programmes existed for supervisors and managers in the investigative field (Stelfox, 2009; Tong et al, 2009; McGrory and Treacy, 2012). Undoubtedly, there have been improvements in terms of investigative development, not least the training of investigation, supervision and management under the auspices of PIP, but these findings suggest problems continue to arise.

The extent to which supervision and management occurs in reality is open to question, even in the modern era. Specific recording mechanisms are available for officers to document their investigative rationale. In volume crime cases, this is usually within the electronic copy of the crime report (CoP, 2016a). In a major crime, this is usually by way of entries into a policy file. Serious and complex crimes are either recorded on the crime report or within a policy file, depending on complexity and seriousness and the judgement of the investigator (CoP, 2016a). These would appear to be ideal places for supervisors and managers to record evidence of their active supervision or management. APP specifically suggests that supervisors document an investigation plan for investigators to pursue as a minimum. Interestingly, figures in this study suggest failure to record an investigative rationale in 12% of the cases in the earlier time period, and 4.5% of cases in the later time period. This implies an improvement in the practice of recording rationale, although further study would be fruitful in understanding whether this process is embedded in modern investigative practice. The recording of rationale is liable to assist an investigator in thinking through their investigations, thereby conducting them in a more thorough and professional fashion. Unfortunately, recording is often seen as a means to assist memory (CoP, 2016a) or to 'cover one's back', rather than a means through which to consider the investigation and its focus as it is ongoing. O'Neill (2011) asked investigators why some cases were sub-standard. Lack of supervision was the second most-cited reason (27%). In addition, the same officers were asked what prevents investigative failure. Good supervision was the most important factor, highlighted by 36% of respondents.

Some cases (in both time periods) lacked proactive supervision in the early stages of investigations in order to ensure that appropriate lines of enquiry were pursued. Such proactivity would seem more important in cases of vulnerability, where previous evidence has suggested that there is a greater risk of harm should failings occur (i.e. DA, missing persons). That said, there may be other reasons why supervision and management is lacking in some of these high-profile cases. As we saw from the research of Turnbull and Wass (2015), in austerity, particularly at Inspector rank, extreme working becomes the norm, potentially leading to overwork, fatigue and consequent error.

Lack of experience

Lack of experience was highlighted as an issue in 19% of cases in the earlier time period, but only in 2% of cases in the later time frame. This could provide implicit support for PIP. Since its inception in 2005, the framework has delineated crimes and investigator development on the basis of crime seriousness. The PIP levels identify the crime seriousness a particular officer is qualified to investigate. The nature of policing is such that sometimes the exigencies of duty will require an officer to investigate above or below their qualification level (James and Mills, 2012), but the framework exists to ensure that this is minimised as much as possible.

Resources

In relation to lack of resources, this has not just been the product of austerity. Scarce resources against the backdrop of increased demand have been identified in both uniformed response and detective work in the UK (Chatterton and Bingham, 2007; Chatterton, 2008; O'Neill, 2011). There is evidence from the Chatterton study that suggests this has an effect on the quality of service to the public. Chatterton (discussing his earlier study of uniformed response officers: Chatterton and Bingham, 2007), stated:

> Response officers acknowledged that the volume and intensity of incidents they are required to attend means that they do not have time to investigate those incidents as thoroughly as they should. They told us that evidence is lost because of delays in responding to reported incidents and because they are under constant pressure from control centres and their first line supervisors to move quickly to the next incident. (Chatterton, 2008, p 29)

Officers reported frustration in not producing a good service to the public, and this poor service consequently had a detrimental effect on detective work, particularly where early evidence was lost by poor initial response. Similarly, Chatterton (2008) found GOCID frustrated at an inability to do a good job due to under-resourcing. O'Neill (2011) asked investigators why some cases were sub-standard. The most commonly cited reason was lack of time (30%), but lack of resources was also cited as a major factor (24%). This, like Chatterton's study, was *before* austerity. With the advent of austerity and further cutbacks, it would be surprising if such a situation has improved. Lack of resources was highlighted by the IPCC as a feature in over one quarter of cases in the earlier time period, yet in the later time period (the austerity period) that figure had *reduced* to 14%. This despite studies highlighting officers concerns that reduced resources would affect their service to the public (Hoggett et al, 2014), and identifying higher workload, particularly in CID management posts (Turnbull and Wass, 2014). The IPCC has in the past commented on the potential effect of high workloads on performance and individual errors, but in most cases observe that failings are individual rather than organisational (see, for instance, IPCC, 2014). In a bulletin of 1 June 2007, the IPCC suggested that failings in DA cases was sometimes rooted in lack of resources (IPCC, 2007). Lack of resources and the overwork of staff have also been commented on in the second time period. See, for instance, comments made by the IPCC about the workload of inspectors in the Arsema Dawit investigation (IPCC, 2010c).

Laziness

While 'laziness' is both a subjective and pejorative term liable to be destructive rather than constructive, it is potentially an aspect of cases in both time periods. Indeed, it was highlighted by investigators as a cause of failed cases in the O'Neill (2011) study. When asked to identify why some cases were sub-standard, officers cited laziness (18%) among possible explanations. When asked why cases fail, laziness was cited in 14% of responses. Modern practitioners *do* recognise laziness in other investigators, identifying how some do not investigate crimes as thoroughly as they should, and how that can affect case outcomes (O'Neill, 2011). Unfortunately, the study did not ask respondents what *types* of cases they felt peers displayed laziness in. It would have been interesting to see whether they felt that laziness was indiscriminate or whether certain types of cases produced such behaviour. Also, as the study was between 2008 and 2011, an interesting question is whether current investigators identify laziness as an issue in austerity. Lack of time is an area that has been identified in the past as a contributory factor in poor police interviews (Kebbell and Milne, 1998; Fisher et al, 1987). In terms of what makes an investigation go wrong, issues such as poor organisational skills, lack of attention to detail and poor communications featured near the top of officers' perceptions.

Failure to carry out even the most fundamental investigations, in the absence of any mitigating circumstances, is arguably a feature of many of the reported IPCC investigations. Whether mitigation exists in terms of other factors not mentioned (i.e. fatigue, low morale, time pressures, or other organisational stressors (Shane, 2010)), is another matter, and could only be ascertained by further research, including interviews with officers and staff deemed to have performed to an inadequate standard. It is important to clarify that there are few IPCC cases where guilt on the part of the officer or staff member is conclusively established. In a large number of cases, the IPCC makes recommendations to the relevant police force in terms of misconduct, poor performance or no further action. If an individual is subject to misconduct proceedings, they may be exonerated following a full examination of evidence. The cases dealt with in this study therefore reflect the opinions of the IPCC following investigation; they do not represent final determinations of police disciplinary processes, or criminal courts. .

Laziness is not a term used by the IPCC to describe officer conduct, and this is understandable, as IPCC reports will often precede any CPS referral, coroner's inquest, or disciplinary action taken against officers and staff for failings (IPCC, 2016). However, some of the failings evident in the published reports would arguably merit exactly that conclusion because seemingly basic investigative tasks have not been undertaken and there appear to be few reasons why this has not been the case. Cases relating to laziness are distinct from those cases where mitigation is apparent in terms of genuine mistake, lack of resources, work overload, and lack of experience in the role. Support for the laziness theme could be said to come from findings suggesting that in the earlier time period, nearly half of recommendations related to 'reminding' officers and staff of existing law, policy and procedure, while in the second time period, nearly one quarter of recommendations suggested the same. Reminding officers suggests that they already knew, or should have known, of the existence of law, policies, practices or procedures, although that too would depend on the amount of training and awareness provided to staff. It has been suggested that police see the provision of training (particularly e-learning packages through NCALT), as a means by which the police organisation can assist disciplinary proceedings against officers and staff should they come under investigation. This would be so even if they were trained in what they suggest is a superficial and ineffective manner (Honess, 2016). Difficulties arise in trying to determine exact causes for failings. While a single reason might be the cause within some poor investigations, there may be numerous reasons in others. Moreover, some investigations highlight failings by a number of individuals rather than a single person. Without further detailed analysis in relation to context, firm conclusions are difficult.

Worryingly, many of the failings appear to relate to vulnerability. For instance, cases either where a complainant is potentially at risk or where they are reporting a serious sexual offence to the police. There are suggestions that police officers may very well view these cases, victims and situations in a more negative light (Christie, 1986) or view the cases as inherently problematic and unworthy of attention (Tong et al, 2009). Lack of management and supervision was highlighted in individual failings in 28% of the earlier time period, compared to 17% in the later time period. If, as these figures suggest, supervision and management of investigations is improving, why has the figure relating to poor investigations remained fairly consistent? Further difficulties arise in trying to determine exact causes for the failings. While one reason may be the case within some investigations, there may be multiple reasons in others. Without further detail in relation to the context, conclusions are again difficult.

Training

Organisationally, there were consistent calls in both time periods to train or further train officers and staff. A majority of these recommendations for further training related to domestic abuse and associated risk assessments. If training is a consistent problematic over two six-year periods, one has to question the relevance of the training or consider whether changes to training (if they occur as a result of learning lessons) merely deal with the specific training issue raised rather than with underlying problems. This supports somewhat the criticisms by Waddington (2015), and Owers (NPCC, 2016) in relation to how police appear to learn lessons by placing a sticking plaster over each problem without ever dealing with systematic issues. This factor is complicated by the fact that there is no single police service in EW, but a number of localised forces. IPCC investigation reports may make organisational recommendations at both national and local levels. Any local recommendations and requisite learning will only be considered relevant by that particular BCU or Police Force, unless the issue is deemed by the IPCC to have wider implications. In the organisational recommendations from both time periods, there were 16 national recommendations from a combined total of 281. The others were labelled 'local' issues. In fairness, this does not take into account areas considered significant enough by the IPCC to include in their learning lessons bulletins. In domestic abuse investigations, lack of training has also been raised by practitioners themselves (HMIC, 2015b). This leads directly to the next problematic area identified by this study.

Risk assessment in domestic abuse cases

The findings are suggestive of major issues in relation to risk assessment of vulnerable missing persons, domestic abuse (DA) victims and those subject to threats to life, with the large majority of cases relating to risk assessment in DA cases. Criticisms of police responses to DA are not new (HMIC, 2014b). DA cases now make up just over 10% of the total reported crime in EW (excluding fraud cases). In the year 2015–16 alone, over 421,000 crimes relating to DA were recorded by the police, with interpersonal violence accounting for 335,000 of those calls. The number of DA incidents recorded by police was over 1 million (ONS, 2016). Put into perspective, each call demands a police response, that police conduct investigations, and assessment in order to consider the risk to the complainant. While dealing with DA is a complex process to manage within the police and in conjunction with other agencies (Stanley and Humphreys, 2014), and clearly not just the responsibility of the police, it is as first responders to DA cases that the police are in a unique and difficult position of needing to gather appropriate information to inform a thorough risk assessment, and seek evidence that might assist proof of criminal offences where appropriate. In relation to risk, it has been identified that: 'Risk assessments are only as good as the information that informs them' (Stanley and Humphreys, 2014, p 80).

That said, they are also only useful as preventative measures if they are:

- appropriate instruments on which to rely,
- well understood by staff who have been trained sufficiently to gather sufficient information and utilise the tool, and
- effectively analysed by suitably trained staff (Richards et al, 2008; Humphreys et al, 2005).

In theory at least, each police force should have appropriate risk assessment protocols, well-trained staff and a professional approach to dealing with such cases. This is so particularly when the latest figures reported by Refuge (2016) suggest that at least two women are killed each week by a current or former partner. While it is clear that the police cannot be held responsible for the criminal acts of others, they can play an essential part in prevention with an appropriate response to reports. In addition, this responsibility to prevent and protect sometimes dovetails into threat-to-life issues and the duties that authorities have to protect life under Article 2 of the Human Rights Act (Osman v United Kingdom, 1998).

Many of the cases reported in this study present a less than flattering picture of the overall police response. For example, the IPCC were critical of Nottinghamshire Police response to the incidents that ultimately led to the murder of Casey Brittle by her partner (IPCC, 2011a). Criticising the police response to the case, the IPCC went on to observe that the force had failed to heed the lessons of a case that occurred in 2009 (Gail Hdili) where similar issues arose (IPCC, 2010a). In the IPCC report into the Essex police handling of the circumstances that led to the murders of Christine and Shania Chambers, the IPCC were critical that the force had not heeded lessons from both IPCC and internal reviews about under-resourcing of departments (IPCC, 2012). In 2013, the IPCC investigation into GMPs handling of reports prior to the murder of Katie Cullen resulted in criticism of the force for failing to heed lessons from previous recommendations for both GMP and other forces in relation to responses to DA (IPCC, 2013b). In that report, the IPCC observed that following three cases that occurred in 2008 and 2009 (Katie Boardman, Katie Cullen and Clare Wood (2010b; 2013b), GMP stated that they had learned lessons and made improvements to practice. The IPCC were concerned therefore to discover that in 2014, GMP was one of four forces highlighted as needing remedial action to improve their response to DA reports (IPCC, 2013b). These cases tend to support Waddington's assertion that the police simply do not learn the lessons even if they say they do. Commenting that the police response to domestic abuse was simply not good enough, HMIC stated: 'Domestic abuse is a priority on paper but, in the majority of forces, not in practice' (HMIC, 2014b, p 6). They went on to observe that risk identification required urgent attention to ensure protection of DA victims, criticising a tick-box mentality for obscuring the objective of police involvement. (HMIC, 2014b, p 6).

This discussion demonstrates a real issue with learning lessons. Looking back to one of the earliest *Learning lessons* bulletins, comments by the IPCC in relation to DA can be compared to the modern era Strikingly, similar issues are being identified more than a decade later: 'Key lessons are the need for better training in domestic violence and proactive management, based on greater awareness of risk factors; to ensure ownership of policies and investigatory procedures by those responsible for implementing them; for processes to identify potential critical incidents and ensure referral to the command team' (IPCC, 2007, p 3).

In 2015, HMIC published a further report on the police response to DA (HMIC, 2015b). They found that some steps had been taken to improve responses, including provision of further training, increased supervision, and the use of a mnemonic (THRIVE) to try to encourage staff to respond to incident reports by concentrating on Threat, Harm, Risk, Investigation, Vulnerability and Engagement. However, even 'good' innovations such as THRIVE were sometimes being utilised to justify *limited* response rather than as a tailored response to the victim's needs. What was evident was the need for good leadership, coupled with a need to ensure that staff understood the reasoning for such innovations.

Worryingly, HMIC (2017) recently found that police reclassified high-risk victims of DA because they had a shortage of officers. While this is a pragmatic response to austerity, it represents risky tactics in an area where police claim to have learnt lessons from past mistakes. Robinson et al (2016) conducted research into the risk factors considered by police officers to be most relevant to their perceptions of domestic abuse. Observing that officers tended to concentrate on a small number of risk factors, to the exclusion of others, the authors identified poor understanding among officers of the importance of risk assessment (and the risk factors), as well as poor and uneven training. Once again, an increased quantity and quality of training was recommended.

Carson et al (2013) approach the discussion of public protection and risk from a different perspective. They argue that these problems are 'wicked' problems, as distinct from tame problems. Wicked problems require leadership rather than command and control, tick-box strategies, because of the inherent difficulty in detailing one 'best' option. The authors suggest that previous responses to wicked problems tended to be process driven and specific. Such responses, with a one-size-fits-all mentality, eliminate professional discretion. Carson et al (2013) posit a more flexible, supportive approach. These are interesting considerations, bearing in mind the lack of improved practice over time, and they provide support for those who have championed an increase in professional discretion rather than a strict regime of policies and practices. Whether increased discretion is the appropriate response is debatable, bearing in mind the history of poor practice, and any development in this regard would need to be on the basis that police education and training was such that the professionals had sufficient knowledge and understanding to be able to make such judgements. Even then, failings sometimes point to a deeper problem than failure to adhere to policies and practices. The Colette Lynch investigation noted:

The second simple theme is that it is never sufficient to adopt 'good practice' in a formal and well intentioned manner by policy resolution. The purpose of a policy and the human consequences of failing to internalise its importance must be born in on all of those entrusted with its implementation by and from the senior management downwards. (IPCC, 2006, p 7)

A failure to understand the importance of the issues involved, coupled with a poor attitude, have been highlighted by inspections (HMIC, 2015b) as well as research (Robinson et al, 2016).

Conclusion

The preliminary findings reported in this study identify some key themes that emerge consistently across a 12-year period. None of the findings are altogether surprising. The fact that training and 'reminding officers' is a consistent theme is a real concern, particularly as that period also saw the implementation of the PIP process to professionalise investigations and a move to utilise technology for training. It raises some legitimate questions as to the effectiveness of PIP as a regime, and the nature and quality of training programmes attached to it, although consideration also needs to be given to individual motivations, knowledge and professionalism. The specific area of risk assessment and its associated strategic and operational employment also raises questions around the effectiveness of internal policies, training and direction in such a critical area of practice. In 2015, the HMIC reported on developments in police responses to DA since their critical report of 2014 (HMIC, 2015b). They identified some progress by the police in the 21-month period, observing that reported crime had risen (potentially meaning that recording practices had improved), better victim awareness and care on the part of officers, forces determined to make DA a priority in reality rather than on paper, and engagement with outside agencies. Various supportive agencies had also described a marked improvement in policed practice. Adopting a cautionary tone, the HMIC remarked that while improvement was evident, continued improvement was required. Whether these 'new' improvements, after over a decade of failings, reports, recommendations and suffering do indeed represent a new era of response to such cases remains to be seen. An era of fewer resources, greater demand, increased stress, high workload and more reliance on abstract learning and development is unlikely to deliver the highly professional response to DA that the public deserves. It must be stressed that the total elimination of failings in cases, like the elimination of MOJs, is a romantic notion that cannot survive reality. An aspiration, undoubtedly, but a realistic notion? Probably not. The best that can be hoped is that fully committed, competent professionals, are able to utilise law, policy and practice to its best effect in serving the public, and that in that endeavour they do their very best. When the professionals have been supported in their development by high-quality education and training, and policies, practices and procedures that impact on their work are clear and consistent, they should be supported even if they occasionally make the wrong decision, especially given the current resource issues that undoubtedly pervade. There is evidence of police change and the promise of further change, although one is still left with the feeling that the rhetoric does not yet reflect practice. The paucity of quality training and the over-reliance on e-learning in relation to DA also defies logic considering the number of times DA and risk assessments have been problematic in the past. The police have an undeniably difficult task to perform and their capacity to cope with demand has been reduced, with officers carrying larger-than-ever caseloads. The themes identified here, such as poor training, poor supervision and management, poor response to certain crimes, lack of resourcing, laziness, and poor risk assessment in DA cases in particular, appear to recur time and again. Systems and processes appear to change, as does the rhetoric, yet practice does not appear to do so. In that sense, Waddington's observation appears to have some merit.

Further reading

Porter, L.E. and Prenzler, T. (2012) 'Police oversight in the United Kingdom: the balance of independence and collaboration'. *International Journal of Law, Crime and Justice*, 40(3): 152–71.

Robinson, A.L., Pinchevsky, G.M., and Guthrie, J.A. (2016) 'A small constellation: risk factors informing police perceptions of domestic abuse'. *Policing and Society*, doi:10.1080/10439463.2016.1151881, 1–16.

Smith, G. (2009) 'Citizen oversight of independent police services: bifurcated accountability, regulation creep, and lesson learning'. *Regulation and Governance*, 3(4): 421–41.

EIGHT

Concluding remarks

This volume has attempted to provide a snapshot of investigative practice in EW in the modern era, how it has evolved historically and how it has attempted to shape itself in austerity and beyond. We have seen how investigation of crime has developed since its early days, from a mythical calling of the few skilled detective artisans, to a new era of investigators at every level of crime seriousness, from uniformed officers dealing with high-volume crime, detectives dealing with serious and complex crime and more specialist officers investigating major criminality. The world has moved on in the 185 years since the official detectives of the New Police were formed.

Research has shed light on investigative practice. The RAND study punctured the myth of effectiveness of detective work and led to a better understanding of what solved crimes and, in some cases, what did not. Screening processes developed over time to ensure that effort was not wasted on volume crime investigations. In EW, over time, uniformed officers became the mainstay of volume crime investigations, while detectives focused on the more serious crimes. PIP was designed to ensure that professional development was in line with case seriousness. The craft mentality, a belief that investigators are somehow born with the skills to be effective, that such skills cannot be taught, and that experience is all, seemingly gave way to a more pragmatic understanding that investigators *can* be taught the rudiments of the profession, although the dominance of craft still prevails. Moreover, recent pronouncements by CoP relating to PIP development appear to signal a return to craft dominance seemingly for reasons of cost (O'Neill, in press)

The Desborough Committee (1920) limited the development of detective practices for decades by pronouncing that criminal investigation was a simple task capable of being performed by citizens in uniform who had no need for specialist training providing they had adequate training in their probationary period. Maybe in those early years, crime investigation was less complex. Modern rules of evidence, a proliferation of criminal law, and new and developing strategies by which criminals commit crime (including cybercrime), and a further complex set of policies and procedures all serve to ensure that modern investigative practice is far from simple. That said, a large proportion of volume crimes are either filed without investigation or investigated by uniformed officers. Volume crime investigators have basic training at the lowest level of PIP. Crime management processes ensure that only cases with a chance of success are disseminated for staff to investigate. As Harfield (2008) suggests, as cited in Chapter 1, case screening ensures that limited resources are utilised where they are most likely to succeed. Serious, complex and major crimes are not subject to the same process and require investigators trained at higher PIP levels than those dealing with volume crime. The personnel at these higher PIP levels are entitled to be seen as specialist investigators under PIP, although we have seen in Chapter 3 that more independent research is required to assess whether PIP represents the gold standard of professional practice that its proponents proclaim. The small study by James and Mills (2012) suggests otherwise, although that study was limited to one police force area.

The PIP framework promises much, but no independent studies of its effectiveness exist. The only study in existence is by James and Mills (2012), and this demonstrates tensions between the rhetoric and reality of investigative development. Stelfox (2009) contended that more work was required to embed PIP, otherwise the process would merely reflect a tick-box exercise rather than real professional development. Other studies hint at the tension between practitioners and top-down change. Even the ethical values central to the NDM have failed to be assimilated into practice, born of a lack of respect for CoP, the professional body for policing (Lax, 2014). The Lax study was confined to one force, yet it does raise questions about the effectiveness of police change processes and the extent to which practitioners respect their own professional body. Fahsing and Ask (2016) lament the absence of PIP in Norway, and while PIP in the UK is an improvement on previous practice, it requires investment from cultural, managerial and financial perspectives, otherwise it is in danger of resembling a cosmetic exercise to appease the public without making any difference to professional practice. Pronouncements by CoP (2013) of a return to craft dominance in investigator development do not bode well for the future, unless there is a bridge to evidence based research and what Willis and others (Willis, 2013; Willis and Mastrofski, 2016) see as essential partnership between craft and science.

The way in which police officers attain and retain their investigative skills requires further research too. In an era of evidence-based practice, it is surprising to find little research on the nature of legal training, how e-learning works in relation to investigative practice, and whether investigators at all levels have sufficient depth of legal knowledge to be able to effectively ply their trade. This links to Chapter 5, which specifically asks whether legal education has become secondary to skills training to the point where law knowledge is neglected. There is evidence from the HMIC and HMCPSI joint inspection that police knowledge of law is lacking, and a call by that report to ensure better knowledge of law on the part of the police. The IPCC research in Chapter 7 would suggest that a large percentage of high-profile cases contain failings relating either to lack of knowledge of the law, or a failure to take it into consideration when undertaking investigations. Recommendations for further training or 'reminding staff of their training' suggest a discord between training and its operationalisation of that training, although reasons for this are difficult to discern.

The centrality of law to effective investigative practice is undeniable. That is not to say that law enforcement is the only effective police response to incidents, as POP and other evidence-based approaches demonstrate (Goldstein, 1990). Even POP, however, requires a response that considers a range of options, including law enforcement. Any response by necessity requires knowledge of legal powers, when it is appropriate to engage the law, or when it is reasonable *not* to invoke the full powers of the criminal law. Discretion in any sense requires knowledge and competence if it is to be applied correctly. Chapter 5 asks whether police officers are educated appropriately in term of both the importance of the rule of law (and adherence to it) and the practical application of that law to effective investigative practice. As well as demonstrating how the law has in the past been used in a negative fashion, the chapter sought to demonstrate ways in which knowledge of the law can inform effective practice. Some examples were considered, although all investigative practice is capable of being informed in the same way. The proliferation of distance learning, e-learning and a stated return to craft development, absent formal training and education, risks failure to embed evidence-based law into practice. Admittedly, the developments in relation to the use of technology in training are artefacts of modernity, and are utilised in other educational fields. However, without the practical application, law taught in an abstract may fail to embed into effective practice. The use of e-learning to train officers in critical areas of practice (i.e. DA) has been subject to IPCC criticism, and the small study by Honess (2016) revealed dissatisfaction not only in relation to the nature and quality of training packages, but also disquiet over the use made of training records through NCALT whenever disciplinary matters arise.

Investigative decision-making is an area of both interest and concern. Chapter 4 suggests that too little regard has been given to investigative decision-making, especially given its links to MOJs and case failures. Since the two Royal Commissions, some steps have been taken to try to improve the open-minded approach of investigators. Changes to interview practice have had some effect on this, and the MIM and CD can be seen as attempts to provide guidance in how best to investigate both major crime and other crime. CD in particular was meant to signal the beginning of a research agenda to improve investigative practice even further. On that, and CPD to support PIP progression, the service has failed. In an era of evidence-based practice, there is a surprising lack of independent research to support the NDM as the core model for police decision-making. Does the NDM really represent a one-size-fits-all model capable of being utilised for all decisions within policing? Born as it was from the CMM, it is doubtful that it has utility within the complexities of modern investigative decision-making. Undoubtedly, practitioners have attempted to embed the model in their everyday practice, but does it help or hinder through the breadth of volume, serious and major crime investigations, and indeed do practitioners actually use it?

There is conflict too between the professional discretion posited by CoP and how this links to increased professionalism. On the one hand, current thinking champions greater use of professional judgement, even in relation to proportionate recording of decisions made. On the other hand, one could argue that such professional independence and increased discretion requires proof of knowledge and competence currently lacking in some police practitioners. That is not to say it is the fault of practitioners either. Training, qualifications and standards in a profession need to be high, instead of based on a lowest common denominator and driven by financial considerations. Allowing further autonomy without a true professional infrastructure allows an organisation to step away from blame, leaving the practitioner responsible (Heaton, 2009). Recent pronouncements from CoP and the IPCC tend to promote proportionality, seemingly on the basis that the term only reflects seriousness of offence. In effect, it appears to suggest that the less serious the case, the less investigative effort can be applied to it. In fact the less serious the case, the greater the professional judgement that can be applied, meaning that an officer can decide whether to record decisions at all. This debate is exacerbated by austerity. With a burgeoning workload allied to fewer resources, professional discretion is likely to have a default position of doing the bare minimum in relation to both thoroughness and recording of investigative decisions. Rather than encouraging professional practice, such autonomy risks returning the police to a less professional state, unless training, education and CPD is meaningful. Undoubtedly, poor practice has a negative effect on police legitimacy and accountability.

Studies on the effects of austerity are limited, and those that exist can be dismissed (incorrectly) as partisan. Some studies in Chapter 2 point to resource issues, work overload, increased sickness, low morale and decreased effectiveness. Some of these issues were identified *before* austerity (see Chatterton's 2008 study of GOCID), but there is little reason to believe that the situation has improved in austerity. Indeed the recent HMIC report confirms under-resourcing within the investigative function. Respondents in the James and Mills study suggest that working in CID is no longer an attractive proposition. Further research would be useful to determine why officers currently turn away from an investigative role (despite suggested reasons proffered by Sir Tom Winsor recently). With current under-resourcing of detective posts, investigative roles will still need to be filled. If officers do not volunteer, there is a risk that some will be 'press-ganged' into the role. Some may even enjoy the role once there, but others will not, with consequent problems of low morale and demotivation. The ideas of direct entry detectives (MPS) and streamlining identified officers into detective posts is a step forward, but it again raises the issue of what standards are applied to recruitment and training of detectives. There is little knowledge of what makes an effective investigator in modernity, so any criterion utilised risks returning to once-accepted myths and stereotypes. Direct-entry detective schemes would benefit from research alongside emerging programmes. Such a process could ensure that any modern scheme does not go the same way as similar schemes of the past (Shpayer-Makov, 2011).

It is not a new finding that risk assessment in DA cases is problematic, and we have seen how the sheer number of DA incidents the police are called on to respond to is extremely high. There is support for a move away from a prescriptive approach in such cases, with a suggestion that a tick box mentality (i.e. DASH risk assessment) should be replaced by more discretion and professional judgement. Carson et al (2013) in particular suggest that risk problems in public protection are less liable to be dealt with properly by a 'top-down' command-and-control mentality than with a more flexible reliance on professional judgement. This, they argue, is the nature of certain 'wild' problems such as domestic abuse. Again, reliance on professional discretion assumes competence, training, education, capacity and support, facets that are arguably underdeveloped within the modern service. The issue of police response to vulnerability and public protection produces tensions with case seriousness. While there is a pragmatic approach to crime seriousness due to scarce resources, vulnerable people are victims of crime at all levels. In some cases, police have responded to low-level incidents without identifying vulnerability. This has resulted in sometimes tragic outcomes (IPCC, 2011b). As a result, some forces are currently structuring their response to incidents with the issue of vulnerability at its core (see Kent Police, 2017).

On a final note, the increased demand for police to investigate historical sexual offences, together with a rise in crime enhanced by the use of technology really does seem to be placing an extra burden on an already stretched resource. Is it any wonder that cracks are beginning to show and evidence is emerging of corner-cutting, high sickness rates, and more investigative failings? The picture painted is bleak, and it does not bode well for a system that prides itself on trying to prevent MOJs from occurring. There appears to be fertile ground for MOJs to flourish under these emerging conditions.

What should be evident from this volume is that great strides have been taken in the field of criminal investigation, and as a result of research, improved practice, science, the capturing of craft, and legislation, modern practice is some way forward from early incarnations of police investigators. The increased complexity of crime and criminality, together with the technological advances that have revolutionised modern times, mean that there is little time to stand still. As criminals develop, so too must the technology, investigative skills and effectiveness of investigations. Evidence-based policing promises much, but it is yet to be seen how such evidence embeds into practice, whether it has capacity to inform practice nationwide, and to what extent research considered valid remains relevant over time. Policing research is encouraged from within the police, from the ground up, practitioner-led, while academic research from outside, divorced from practitioners, appears to be the new pariah. While the blending of craft and science is to be encouraged, research outside this focus should also be encouraged. When the service encourages professionalisation; when police HE degrees are fêted as the way ahead; when PIP is held up as an exemplary framework; when the NDM is posited as a one-size-fits-all decision-making model for policing; and when other changes are made seemingly on the grounds of improvement, research is entitled to question the evidence base for such developments, and whether those questions arise from research within or outside the service is irrelevant as long as questions continue to be asked. This acts as another necessary form of accountability and legitimacy. If you have read to the end of this volume, thank you for your time. I encourage you to read further and explore the world of books journals and materials that exist in relation to both policing and criminal investigations. Grabosky (2012) once observed that criminal investigation was 'a mansion with many rooms'. Thus far, many of the rooms appear to be unexplored and little understood.

References

ACPO (2001) *Volume Crime Investigation Manual*. London: ACPO Crime Committee.

ACPO (2005) *MIRSAP manual: Major incident room standard administrative procedures*. Wyboston: NPIA.

ACPO (2006) *Murder investigation manual*. Wyboston: NPIA.

ACPO (2009a) *Practice advice on the management of priority and volume crime*, 2nd edn. Wyboston: NPIA.

ACPO (2009b) Guidance on command and control. Wyboston: NPIA. Available at: www.ipcc.gov.uk/sites/default/files/Documents/acpo_guidance_on_command_and_control_-_2009-2.pdf

ACPO, Centrex (2005) *Practice advice on core investigative doctrine*. Wyboston: Association of Chief Police Officers and National Policing Improvement Agency.

Adams, R.F. (2014) 'Does the police service need a values-based decision-making model: if so, what should that model look like?' Unpublished master's thesis, London Metropolitan University.

Allsop, C. (2013) Motivations, money and modern policing: accounting for cold case reviews in an age of austerity. *Policing and Society*, volume 23(3), pp.362-375.

Anti-social Behaviour, Crime and Policing Act, 2014. London: HMSO.

Ariza, J.J.M., Robinson, A. and Myhill, A. (2016) 'Cheaper, faster, better: expectations and achievements in police risk assessment of domestic abuse'. *Policing*, 10(4) 341–50. DOI: 10.1093/police/paw023.

Ashworth, A. (2000) 'Is the criminal law a lost cause?' *Law Quarterly Review*, 116(2): 225–56.

Ask, K. and Granhag, P.A. (2005) 'Motivational sources of confirmation bias in criminal investigations. The need for cognitive closure'. *Journal of Investigative Psychology and offender Profiling*, 2(1): 43–63.

Audit Commission (1993) *Helping with enquiries: Tackling crime effectively*. London: HMSO.

Auld, L.J. (2001) *A review of the criminal courts in England and Wales*. Final report. London: HMSO.

Baldwin, J. (1992) *Video-taping of police interviews with suspects: An evaluation*. Police Research Series: Paper No. 1. London: Home Office.

Baldwin, J. (1993) 'Police interview technique – establishing truth or proof?' *British Journal of Criminology*, 33, 325–51.

Baldwin, J. and Moloney, T. (1992) *Supervision of police investigation in serious criminal cases*. Royal Commission on Criminal Justice, Research Study no. 4. London: HMSO.

Bayley, D.H. (2002) 'Law enforcement and the rule of law: is there a trade off?' *Criminology and Public Policy*, 2(1): 133–54.

Bayley, D.H. and Bittner, E. (1984) 'Learning the skills of policing'. *Law and Contemporary Problems, Discretion in Law Enforcement*, 47(4): 35–59.

BBC (2006) 'Rape on Trial', BBC1, *Panorama*, Sunday 25 June. Transcript available at: http://news.bbc.co.uk/1/hi/programmes/panorama/4784743.stm

Beattie, J.M. (2012) *The first English detectives: The Bow Street Runners and the policing of London, 1750–1840*. Oxford: Oxford University Press.

Bell, N.R.A. and Wood, A. (2015) *Howard Vincent's Police Code, 1889*. London: Mango Books.

Benson, M.S., and Powell, M.B. (2015) Evaluation of a comprehensive interactive training system for investigative interviewers of children. *Psychology, Public Policy, and Law*, 21(3): 309–22.

Berger, P.L., and Luckmann, T. (1966). *The social construction of reality*. New York: Doubleday.

Berry, J. (2010) *Reducing bureaucracy in policing*. Final report, October 2010. Available at: www.gov.uk/government/uploads/system/uploads/attachment_data/file/117162/reduce-bureaucracy-police.pdf.

Bichard, M. (2004) *The Bichard inquiry report*. London: The Stationery Office.

Bingham, T. (2011) *The rule of law*. London: Penguin.

Bloch, P., and Weidman, D. (1976) *Managing criminal investigations*. Washington, DC: National Institute of Law Enforcement and Criminal Justice.

Bottomley, K. and Coleman, C. (1981) *Understanding crime rates*. Farnborough: Gower.

Brandl, S.G., and Horvath, F. (1991) 'Crime-victim evaluation of police investigative performance'. *Journal of Criminal Justice*, 19: 293–305.

Brodeur, J.P. (2010) *The policing web*. Oxford: Oxford University Press.

Brodeur, J.P., and Dupont, B. (2006) 'Knowledge workers or "knowledge" workers?' *Policing and Society*, 16(1): 7–26.

Brogden, M. and Ellison, G. (2013) *Policing in an age of austerity: A post-colonial perspective*. Abingdon: Routledge.

Brookman, F. (2005) Understanding homicide. London: Sage.

Brookman, F. and Innes, M. (2013) 'The problem of success. What is a good homicide investigation?' *Policing and Society*, 23(3): 292–310.

Brown, M.F. (2001). *Criminal investigation: Law and practice*. Oxford: Butterworth-Heinemann.

Bryant, R.P. (2009a) 'Theories of criminal investigation', in Tong, S., Bryant, R. and Horvath, A. (eds) *Understanding criminal investigation*. Oxford: Wiley Blackwell, pp 13–35.

Bryant, R.P. (2009b) 'Forms of reasoning and the analysis of intelligence in criminal investigation', in Tong, S., Bryant, R. and Horvath, A. (eds) *Understanding criminal investigation*. Oxford: Wiley Blackwell, pp 35–49.

Bryant, R. and Bryant, S. (eds) (2016). Blackstone's Handbook for Policing Students 2016. Oxford University Press.

Bull, R (2014) *Investigative interviewing*. London: Springer.

Burke, A.S. (2006) Improving Prosecutorial Decision Making: Some Lessons of Cognitive Science, *William and Mary Law Review*, 47: 1587–1634.

Burrows, J. and Tarling, R. (1987) 'The investigation of crime in England and Wales'. *The British Journal of Criminology*, 27(3): 229–51. Oxford: Oxford University Press.

Burrows, J., Hopkins, M., Hubbard, R., Robinson, A., Speed, M. and Tilley, N. (2005) *Understanding the attrition process in volume crime investigations*. Home Office Research Study no. 295. London: Home Office Research, Development and Statistics Directorate.

Byford, L. (1981) *Report into the police handling of the Yorkshire Ripper case*. London: Home Office.

Carr, A. F., Schnelle, J.F., Larson, L. D., and Kirchner, J. E. (1980) Outcome Measures of Police Performance: Some Steps Toward Positive Accountability, *Journal Of Community Psychology* , 8 (2): 165–71.

Carson, D. (2007) 'Models of investigation', in Newburn, T., Williamson, T. and Wright, A. (eds) *Handbook of criminal investigation*, pp 407–26. Cullompton, Devon: Willan Publishing.

Carson, D. (2009a) 'The abduction of Sherlock Holmes'. *International Journal of Police Science & Management*, 11(2): 193–202.

Carson, D. (2009b) 'Detecting, developing and disseminating detectives' "creative" skills'. *Policing & Society*, 19(3): 216–25.

Carson, D., Nash, M. and Cuff, S. (2013) 'Responsibility for public protection and related risk decision-making'. *The Police Journal*, 86: 307–20.

Caswell, C. (2014) 'Officer Numbers Now at 2002 Levels', *Police Oracle*. Available at: www.policeoracle.com/news/ HR%2C+Personnel+and+Staff+ Development/2014/Jan/30/ Officer-numbers-now-at-2002-levels_77853.html/news

Cerfontyne, R. (2010) *Andre Hanscombe complaint: Commissioners report*. Available at: www.ipcc.gov.uk/sites/default/files/Documents/investigation_commissioner_reports/hanscombe_complaint_1.pdf

Chan, J. (1996) Changing police culture. *British Journal of Criminology*, 36(1): 109–34.

Chatterton, M. (1995) 'The cultural craft of policing – its past and future relevance'. *Policing and Society*, 5: 97–107.

Chatterton, M. (2008) *Losing the detectives: Views from the front line*. Surbiton: Police Federation of England and Wales.

Chatterton, M. and Bingham, E. (2007) *24/7 response policing in the modern police organisation-views from the frontline*. Surbiton: Police Federation.

Christie, N. (1986) 'The ideal victim', in Fattah, E.A. (ed.) *From crime policy to victim policy*. London: Macmillan, pp 17–30.

Clarke, C. and Milne, R. (2001) *A national evaluation of the PEACE Investigative Interviewing Course*. London: Home Office.

Clarke, C., Milne, R. and Bull, R. (2011) 'Interviewing suspects of crime: The impact of PEACE training, supervision and the presence of a legal advisor'. *Journal of Investigative Psychology and Offender Profiling*, 8(2): 149–62.

Cohen, B. and Chaiken, J.M. (1987) *Investigators who perform well*. US Department of Justice, National Institute of Justice, Office of Communication and Research Utilization. Cambridge, MA: Abt Associates, Inc.

Connor, P., Hutton, G., Johnston, D., McKinnon, G. and Pinfield, D. (2015) *Blackstone's Police Investigators' Manual and Workbook 2016*. Oxford: Oxford University Press.

Cook, T. and Tattersall, A. (2014) *Blackstone's senior investigating officers' handbook*. Oxford: Oxford University Press.

CoP (2013) *Press release relating to forthcoming review of PIP training*. College of Policing.

CoP (2014a) *Code of practice for the principles and standards of professional behaviour for the policing profession of England and Wales*College of Policing. Available at: www.college.police.uk/What-we-do/Ethics/Documents/Code_of_Ethics.pdf

CoP (2014b) PIP *Review Recommendation Report*. College of Policing. Unpublished.

CoP (2015) *Ethics of professional policing*. College of Policing. Available at: www.college.police.uk/What-we-do/Ethics/Documents/Code_of_Ethics.pdf

CoP (2016a) *College of Policing Authorised Professional Practice*. Available at: https://www.app.college.police.uk/

CoP (2016b) *College of Policing CPD Framework*. Available at: www. college.police.uk/What-we-do/Development/professional-development-programme/Documents/CPDFramework.pdf

CoP (2016c) *College of Policing CPD Toolkit*. Available at: www.college. police.uk/What-we-do/Development/professional-development-programme/Pages/CPD_how_-_a_toolkit.aspx

CoP (2017a) *Managing investigations: policy files*. Available at: www. app.college.police.uk/app-content/investigations/managing-investigations/#policy-files

CoP (2017b) *Professionalising the Investigative Process*. Available at: www. college.police.uk/What-we-do/Learning/Professional-Training/Investigation/Documents/PIP_Policy.pdf

CoP/HMIC/IPCC (2014) *Concordat between College of Policing, Her Majesty's Inspectorate of Constabulary and the Independent Police Complaints Commission, June 2014*. Available at: www.ipcc.gov.uk/sites/default/files/Documents/publications/concordat%20HMIC%20COP%20IPCC%201.pdf

CPS (2017) 'Consent', *Rape and sexual offences*. London: CPS. Available at: www.cps.gov.uk/legal/p_to_r/rape_and_sexual_offences/consent/#a03

Crust, P.E. (1975) 'Criminal investigation project'. Home Office Police Research Services Unit (unpublished).

Curtis, I. (2015) *The use of targets in policing*. London: Home Office.

Dean, G. and Gottschalk, P. (2007) *Knowledge management in policing and law enforcement: Foundations, structures, applications*. Oxford: Oxford University Press.

Dean, G., Fahsing, I.A., Gottschalk, P. and Solli-Saether, H. (2008) 'Investigative thinking and creativity: an empirical study of police detectives in Norway'. *International Journal of Innovation and Learning*, 5(2): 170–85.

Desborough, Lord (1920) *Report of the Committee on the Police Service of England and Wales*. London: HMSO.

Devlin, P., Baron (1976) Devlin Committee Report: Report of the Committee on Evidence of Identification in Criminal Cases, 1976 (Cmnd 338) 134/135, 42.

Dicey, A.V. (1959) *An introduction to the study of the law of the constitution*. (10th ed). London: Palgrave Macmillan.

Donovant, B.W. (2009) 'The new, modern practice of adult education: online instruction in a continuing professional education setting'. *Adult Education Quarterly: A Journal of Research and Theory*, 59(3): 227–45.

Eck, J.E. (1983) *Solving crimes: The investigation of burglary and robbery*. Washington, DC: Police Executive Research Forum.

Eck, J. and Spelman, W. (1987) *Problem Oriented Policing in Newport News*. Washington, DC: Police Executive Research Forum.

Ede, R., and Shepherd, E. (2000) *Active defence: A guide to police and defence investigation and prosecution and defence disclosure in criminal cases*. London: The Law Society.

Emsley, C. (2009) *The Great British Bobby. A history of British policing from 1829 to the present*. London: Quercus.

Emsley, C. and Shpayer-Makov, H. (2006) *Police detectives in history, 1750–1950*. Abingdon: Routledge.

Ericson, R.V. (1993) *Making crime: A study of detective work*. Toronto: University of Toronto Press.

Ericson. R.V. and Haggerty, K.D. (1997) *Policing the risk society*. Toronto: University of Toronto Press.

Evans, J.S.B. (1989) *Bias in human reasoning: Causes and consequences*. Mahwah, NJ: Lawrence Erlbaum Associates, Inc.

Fahsing, I.A. (2016) 'The making of an expert detective: Thinking and deciding in criminal investigations'. Unpublished PhD thesis, University of Gothenburg, Sweden.

Fahsing, I.A. and Ask, K. (2013) 'Decision making and decisional tipping points in homicide investigations: an interview study of British and Norwegian detectives'. *Journal of Investigative Psychology and Offender Profiling*, 10(2): 155–65.

Fahsing, I. A. and Ask, K. (2016) 'The making of an expert detective: the role of experience in English and Norwegian police officers' investigative decision-making'. *Psychology, Crime & Law*, 22(3): 203–23.

Fahsing, I.A. and Ask, K. (2017) 'In search of indicators of detective aptitude: police recruits' logical reasoning and ability to generate investigative hypotheses'. *Journal of Police and Criminal Psychology*, doi. org/10.1007/s11896-017-9231-3

Fahsing, I. A. and Gottschalk, P. (2008) 'Characteristics of effective detectives: a content analysis for investigative thinking styles in policing'. *International Journal of Innovation and Learning*, 5(6): 651–63.

Findley, K.A. and Scott, M.S. (2006) 'Multiple Dimensions of Tunnel Vision in Criminal Cases', *The Wisconsin Law Review*, pp 291–398.

Fisher, H. (1977) *Report of an Inquiry By Sir Henry Fisher Into the Circumstances Leading to the Trial of Three Persons on Charges Arising Out of the Death of Maxwell Confait and the Fire at 27 Doggett Road*, London: HM Stationery Office.

Fisher, R.P., Geiselman, R.E. and Raymond, D.S. (1987) 'Critical analysis of police interview techniques', *Journal of Police Science and Administration*, 15(3): 177–85.

Flanagan, Sir R. (2008) *Independent review of policing: final report*. London: Home Office. Available at: http://webarchive.nationalarchives.gov.uk/20080910134927/http://police.homeoffice.gov.uk/publications/police-reform/Review_of_policing_final_report/flanagan-final-report?view=Binary

Forst, B., Lucianovich, J. and Cox, S. (1977) *What happens after arrest?* Promis Research Project, Washington, DC: Institute for Law and Social Research, 4 (August).

Fox, J. (2014) 'Is there room for flair in criminal investigation?' *Journal of Homicide and Major Incident Investigation*, 9(1): 2–18.

Fraser-Mackenzie, P.A. and Dror, I.E. (2009) 'Selective information sampling: cognitive coherence in evaluation of a novel item'. *Judgment and Decision Making*, volume 4(4): 307–16.

Gill, M., Hart, J., Livingstone, K. and Stevens, J. (1996) *The crime allocation system: Police investigation into burglary and auto crime*. Police Research Series, Paper 16. London: Home Office.

Goldstein, J. (1960) 'Police discretion not to invoke the criminal process: Low-visibility decisions in the administration of justice'. *The Yale Law Journal*, 69(4): 543–94.

Goldstein, H. (1990) *Problem oriented policing*. New York: McGraw Hill.

Gorby, D.M. (2013) 'The failure of traditional measures of police performance and the rise of broader measures of performance'. *Policing*, 7(4): 392–400.

Grabosky, P. (2012) 'Criminal investigation: a mansion with many rooms'. *Australian Journal of Forensic Sciences*, 44(10): 1–3.

Green, T. and Gates, A. (2014) 'Understanding the process of professionalization in the police organisation'. *Police Journal of Theory, Practice and Principles*. 87: 75–91.

Greenberg, B., Oliver, S.Y. and Lang, K. (1972) *Enhancement of the investigative function – Volume 1: Analysis and conclusions*. Springfield, VA: National Technical Information Service.

Greenwood, P. (1970) *An analysis of the apprehension activities of the New York City Police Department*. New York: Rand.

Greenwood, P.W. (1979) *The Rand criminal investigation study: Its findings and impacts, to date*. Santa Monica, CA: RAND Corporation.

Greenwood, P., Chaiken, J. and Petersilia, J. (1977) *The criminal investigation process*. Lexington, MA: D.C. Heath.

Gross, H. (1906) *Criminal investigation: A practical handbook for magistrates, police officers, and lawyers*. Madras: A. Krishnamachari.

Guardian (2016) 'Police sick leave for psychological reasons up by a third in five years'. *Guardian*, 5 April. Available at: www.theguardian.com/uk-news/2016/apr/05/police-sick-leave-for-psychological-reasons-up-by-a-third-in-five-years

Guardian (2017) 'Judge criticised over warning to drunk women'. *Guardian*, 11 March. Available at: www.theguardian.com/society/2017/mar/11/judge-criticised-over-warning-to-drunk-women

Gundhus, H.I. (2012) 'Experience or knowledge? Perspectives on new scientific regimens and control of professionalism'. *Policing*, 7(2): 178–94.

HMIC. (2002) *Training Matters*. London: HMIC

HMIC (2004) *Modernising the police service: A thematic inspection of workforce modernisation-the role, management and deployment of police staff in the police service of England and Wales*. London: HMIC.

HMIC (2011) *Demanding times: The front line and police visibility*. London: HMIC

HMIC (2012) *Taking time for crime: A study of how police officers prevent crime in the field*. London: HMIC.

HMIC (2014a) *Policing in austerity: Meeting the challenge*. London: HMIC.

HMIC (2014b) *Everybody's business: Improving the police response to domestic abuse*. London: HMIC.

HMIC (2015a) *PEEL: Police effectiveness 2015 (vulnerability). A national overview*. London: HMIC.

HMIC (2015b) *Increasingly everyone's business: A progress report on the police response to domestic abuse*. IPCC. Available at: www.justiceinspectorates.gov.uk/hmic/wp-content/uploads/increasingly-everyones-business-domestic-abuse-progress-report.pdf

HMIC (2016) 'The state of policing: the annual assessment of policing in England and Wales', 24 February. London: HMIC.

HMIC (2017) *PEEL: Police effectiveness 2016: A national overview*. London: HMIC

HMIC and HMCPSI (2013) *Getting cases ready for court a joint review of the quality of prosecution case files*. July 2013. London: HMIC and HMCPSI.

Hallenberg, K.M. (2012) 'Scholarly detectives: Police professionalisation via academic education'. PhD thesis, University of Manchester.

Hallenberg, K., O'Neill, M. and Tong, S. (2015) 'Watching the detectives', in: Brunger, M and Tong, S. (eds) *Introduction to policing research: Taking lessons from practice*, pp 101–19.

Hammond, J.S., Keeney, R.L. and Raiffa, H. (1998) 'The hidden traps in decision making', *Harvard Business Review*, 76(5): 47–58.

Hardwick, N. (2006) 'The Independent Police Complaints Commission'. *Criminal Justice Matters*, 63(1): 28–9.

Harfield, C. (2008) 'Criminal investigation', in Newburn, T. and Neyroud, P. (eds) *The Dictionary of Policing*. Cullompton: Willan Publishing, pp 67–9.

Hargreaves, J., Cooper, J., Woods, E. and Mckee, C. (2016) 'Police workforce, England and Wales', 31 March. *Statistical Bulletin 05/16*. London: Home Office: Available at: www.gov.uk/government/uploads/system/uploads/attachment_data/file/544849/hosb0516-police-workforce.pdf

Harrison, J. and Cunneen, M. (2000) *An Independent Police Complaints Commission*. London: Liberty.

Hastie, R. and Pennington, N. (1986) 'Evidence evaluation in complex decision-making'. *Journal of Personality and Social Psychology*, 51(2): 242–58.

Hastie, R. and Pennington, N. (1995) 'Cognitive approaches to judgment and decision making'. *Psychology of Learning and Motivation*, 32: 1–31.

Hastie, R. and Pennington, N. (2000) 'Explanation-based decision making', in Connolly, T., Arkes, H.R. and Hammond, K.R. (eds) *Judgment and decision making: An interdisciplinary reader.* Cambridge: Cambridge University Press.

Heaton, R. (2009) 'Police resources, demand and the flanagan report'. *Police Journal*, 82: 95–116.

Heaton, R. (2011) 'We could be criticized! Policing and risk aversion'. *Policing*, 5(1): 75–86.

Henriques, R. (2016) *An Independent Review of the Metropolitan Police Service's handling of non-recent sexual offence investigations alleged against persons of public prominence*, 31 October 2016. Available at: http://news.met.police.uk/documents/report-independent-review-of-metropolitan-police-services-handling-of-non-recent-sexual-offence-investigations-61510

Hobbs, D. (1988) *Doing the business: Entrepreneurship, detectives and the working class in the East End of London*. Oxford: Oxford University Press.

Hoggett, J., Redford, P., Toher, D. and White, P. (2014) *Challenge and change: Police identity, morale and goodwill in an age of austerity*. Technical report. Bristol: University of the West of England.

Holdaway, S. (1983) *Inside the British Police – a force at work*. Oxford: Basil Blackwell.

Home Affairs Committee (2013) *Home Affairs Committee (Eleventh Report): The Independent Police Complaints Commission.* London: HMSO.

Home Office (1993) Circular 17/1993: *Performance indicators for the police.* London: Home Office.

Home Office (2001a) *Justice for all.* Government White Paper. London: Home Office.

Home Office (2001b) *Policing a new century: A blueprint for reform.* London: Home Office.

Home Office (2011) Police Service strength in England and Wales, 31st March 2011. London: Home Office Statistical Bulletin, 11/13, available at: www.gov.uk/government/uploads/system/uploads/attachment_data/file/115757/hosb1311.pdf

Home Office (2016) *Home Office Counting Rules.* Available at: www.gov.uk/government/uploads/system/uploads/attachment_data/file/489732/count-general-january-2016.pdf

Honess, R. (2016) *The mandatory delivery of ongoing training within the police service of England and Wales and its relationship to the andragogical principle of self-motivation.* MSc research thesis, Canterbury Christ Church University. Available at: https://create.canterbury.ac.uk/14999/1/HONESSTHESISv4%20PDF.pdf

Hough, M. (2013) 'Procedural justice and professional policing in times of austerity'. *Criminology and Criminal Justice*, 13(2): 181–97.

House of Commons Home Affairs Committee (2016) 'College of Policing: three years on', Fourth Report of Session 2016–17. London: House of Commons.

Hughes, M. (2011) 'We don't know what the "frontline" is, Home Office admits'. *Telegraph*, 15 March. Available at: www.telegraph.co.uk/news/8383846/We-dont-know-what-the-frontline-is-Home-Office-admits.html

Humphreys, C., Thiara, R.K., Regan, L., Lovett, J., Kennedy, L. and Gibson, A. (2005) *Prevention not prediction: An evaluation of the metropolitan police risk assessment model.* London: Association of Chief Police Officers.

Innes, M. (2003) *Investigating murder: Detective work and the police response to criminal homicide.* Oxford: Oxford University Press.

Innes, M. (2004) 'Signal crimes and signal disorders: notes on deviance as communicative action'. *The British journal of sociology*, 55(3): 335–55.

Innes, M. (2010) 'The art, craft and science of policing', in Cane, P. and Kritzer, H. (eds) *The Oxford handbook of empirical legal research.* Oxford: Oxford University Press, pp 11–36.

Innes, M. (2014) *Signal crimes: Social reactions to crime, disorder, and control.* Oxford: Oxford University Press.

IPCC (2005) *IPCC Annual Report and Accounts 2004/5,* London: IPCC

IPCC (2006) *Investigation into circumstances attendant upon the death of Colette Lynch Commissioner's Executive summary,* pp 1-7. Available at: http://webarchive.nationalarchives.gov.uk/20100908174554/http://www.ipcc.gov.uk/lynch_executive_summary.pdf

IPCC (2007) *Learning the lessons.* Bulletin 1. Available at: www.ipcc.gov.uk/sites/default/files/Documents/learning_the_lessons_bul1june07b.pdf

IPCC (2010a) 'IPCC publish findings from investigation into police contact with Gail Hdili'. 28 October. Available at: www.ipcc.gov.uk/news/ipcc-publish-findings-investigation-police-contact-gail-hdili

IPCC (2010b) *IPCC independent investigation: Greater Manchester Police contact with Clare Wood prior to her death.* 3 October. Available at: www.ipcc.gov.uk/sites/default/files/Documents/investigation_commissioner_reports/clare_wood_report_final_10_march.pdf

IPCC (2010c) *IPCC independent investigation: Police contact between 30 April 2008 and 2 June 2008 with Arsema Dawit and her family. Commissioners report.* October 2010. Available at: www.ipcc.gov.uk/sites/default/files/Documents/investigation_commissioner_reports/dawit_commissioner_s_report.pdf

IPCC (2011a) *Commissioner's report: Investigation into the police management of reports of domestic abuse made by/in relation to Casey Brittle.* Available at: www.ipcc.gov.uk/sites/default/files/Documents/investigation_commissioner_reports/casey_brittle_commissioners_report.pdf

IPCC (2011b) *IPCC report into the contact between Fiona Pilkington and Leicestershire Constabulary 2004–2007.* Available at: www.ipcc.gov.uk/sites/default/files/Documents/investigation_commissioner_reports/pilkington_report_2_040511.pdf

IPCC (2012a) *Christine and Shania Chambers (deceased).* Available at: https://www.ipcc.gov.uk/sites/default/files/Documents/investigation_commissioner_reports/Chambers%20investigation%20report%20summary.PDF

IPCC (2012b) *Complaints made on behalf of Sean Wall against two police officers concerning the handling of TIC's.* Available at: https://www.ipcc.gov.uk/sites/default/files/Documents/investigation_commissioner_reports/Sean_Wall_Commissioners_Report.pdf

IPCC (2013a) *Southwark Sapphire Unit's local practices for the reporting and investigation of sexual offences, July 2008–September 2009*. Available at: www.ipcc.gov.uk/sites/default/files/Documents/investigation_commissioner_reports/Southwark_Sapphire_Units_local_practices_for_the_reporting_and_investigation_of_sexual_offences_july2008_sept2009.PDF

IPCC (2013b) *Investigation into Greater Manchester Police contact with Ms (Redacted) and Ms Katherine Cullen*. Available at: www.ipcc.gov.uk/sites/default/files/Documents/investigation_commissioner_reports/Final%20Report%20CULLEN.pdf

IPCC (2014) *Learning in relation to four incidents of reported Missing Persons/Concern for Safety in the Avon and Somerset Constabulary between the 23rd September 2009 and the 21st April 2010 which resulted in the death of a person in each case*. Available at: https://www.ipcc.gov.uk/sites/default/files/Documents/investigation_commissioner_reports/learning_report_louise_jones_21022014.pdf

IPCC (2016) *Guide to IPCC independent investigations*. Available at: www.ipcc.gov.uk/sites/default/files/Documents/investigation_commissioner_reports/guide_to_IPCC_investigations.pdf

IPCC (2017) *Annual report and statement of accounts*. London: IPCC.

Irving, B. and Dunnighan, C. (1993) *Human factors in the quality control of CID investigations*. Research Study 21. London: HMSO.

Irving, B. and McKenzie, I. (1993) *A Brief Review of Relevant Police Training*. Research Study Number 21, RCCJ, London: HMSO.

Isaacs, H. (1967) 'A study of communications, crimes, and arrests in a metropolitan police department'. *Task Force report: Science and technology*, A Report to the President's Commission on Law Enforcement and Administration of Justice, Washing ton, DC: pp 88–106.

James, A. (2016) *Understanding Police Intelligence Work (Key themes in policing)*. Bristol: Policy Press.

James, A. and Mills, M. (2012) 'Does ACPO know best: to what extent may the PIP programme provide a template for the professionalization of policing?' *The Police Journal*, 85: 133–49.

Jones, B. (2000) 'Why did you decide to do this?' *Policing*, pp 70–9.

Kahneman, D. (2011) *Thinking fast and slow*. London: Penguin Books.

Kassin, S.A., Goldstein, C.C., and Savitsky, K. (2003) 'Behavioral Confirmation in the Interrogation Room: On the Dangers of Presuming Guilt'. *Law and Human Behavior*, Vol. 27, No. 2 (Apr., 2003), pp. 187-203

Kebbell, M.R. and Milne, R. (1998) 'Police officers' perceptions of eyewitness performance in forensic investigations'. *The Journal of social psychology*, 138(3), pp.323-330.

Kent Police (2017) 'New Horizon structure', in *Kent Police Relay*, Special edition, *How far we've come*, 74: 9–10.

Kirby, S. (2013) *Effective policing? Implementation in theory and practice.* London: Palgrave Macmillan.

Klockars, C.B. (1980) 'The dirty Harry problem'. *The annals of the American Academy of Political and Social Science*, 452(1): 33–47.

Kuykendall, J. (1987) 'The municipal police detective: an historical analysis'. *Criminology*, 24(1): 175–202.

Laurie, P. (1970) *Scotland Yard: A study of the Metropolitan Police.* London: Holt Rinehart and Winston.

Lax, M. (2014) 'The affective domain and police values education: is the former used to convey the latter in support of the national decision model?' *Police Journal: Theory Practice and Principles,* 87(2): 126–38.

Laycock, G. (2003) *Launching crime science.* Jill Dando Institute of Crime Science.

Leng, R. and Taylor, R. (1996) *Blackstone's Guide to the Criminal Procedure and Investigations Act 1996.* Oxford: Oxford University Press.

Lepard, D.A. and Campbell, E. (2009) 'How police departments can reduce the risk of wrongful convictions', in Rossmo, K.D. (ed.) *Criminal investigative failures.* Boca Raton, FL: CRC Press, pp 269–93.

Loveday, B. (2008) 'Workforce modernisation in the police service'. *International Journal of Police Science & Management*, 10(2): 136–44.

Loveday, B. (2015) 'Police management and workforce reform in a period of austerity', in Wankhade, P. and Weir, D. (eds) *Police services: Leadership and management perspectives.* Cham: Springer International Publishing, pp 115–27.

Ludwig, A. and Fraser, J. (2014) 'Effective use of forensic science in volume crime investigations: identifying recurring themes in the literature'. *Science & Justice,* 54(1): 81–8.

Lustgarten, L. (1987) 'The police and the substantive criminal law'. *The British Journal of Criminology*, 27(1), *Why Police?: Special Issue on Policing in Britain.* (Winter): 23–30.

Macpherson, W. (1999) *The Stephen Lawrence inquiry: Report of an inquiry by Sir William Macpherson of Cluny.* London: HMSO.

Maguire, M. (2008) 'Criminal investigation and crime control', in Newburn, T. (ed.) *Handbook of Policing*, 2nd edn. Cullompton, Devon: Willan Publishing.

Maguire, M., and Norris, C. (1992) *The conduct and supervision of criminal investigations*. Royal Commission on Criminal Justice: Research Study no. 5. London: HMSO

Maguire, M. and Norris, C. (1994) 'Police investigations: practice and malpractice'. *Journal of Law and Society*, 21(1): 72–84.

Maguire, M., Noaks, C., Hobbs, R. and Brearley, N. (1992) *Assessing investigative performance*. Cardiff: School of Social and Administrative Studies, University of Wales.

Manning, P.K. (1977) *Police work: The social organisation of policing*. Cambridge, MA: MIT Press.

Manning, P.K. (2007) 'Theorizing policing: the drama and myth of crime control in the NYPD'. *Theoretical Criminology*, 5(3): 315–44.

Mason, F. and Lodrick, Z. (2013) 'Psychological consequences of sexual assault'. *Best Practice and Research Clinical Obstetrics & Gynaecology*, 27(1): 27–37.

Matza, D. (1969) *Becoming deviant*. Englewood Cliffs, NJ: Prentice Hall.

McConville, M., Sanders, A. and Leng, R. (1991) *The case for the prosecution: Police suspects and the construction of criminality*. Abingdon: Routledge.

McGrory, D. and Treacy, P. (2012) 'The professionalising investigation programme', in Haberfield, M.R., Clarke, C.A. and Sheridan, D.L. (eds) *Police organisation and training*. London: Springer, pp 113–36.

McGurk, B., Gibson, R. and Platten, T. (1992) *Detectives: A job and training needs analysis*. Harrogate: Central Planning Unit.

Mills, H., Silvestri, A. and Grimshaw, R. (2010) *Police expenditure, 1999–2009*. London: Kings College London: Centre for Crime and Justice Studies.

Milne, R. and Bull, R. (1999) *Investigative interviewing: Psychology and practice*. Chichester: Wiley.

Moore, C.R. and Rubin, G.R. (2014) 'Civilian detective doctrine in the 1930s and its transmission to the military police in 1940–42'. *Law, Crime and History*, pp 1–30. Available at: https://kar.kent.ac.uk/41318/7/Colin%20R%20%20Moore%20and%20Gerry%20R%20%20Rubin%20FINAL.pdf

Morgan, J.B. (1990) *The police function and the investigation of crime*. Brookfield, VT: Avebury.

Morris, B (2007) 'History of criminal investigation', in Newburn, T., Williamson, T. and Wright, A. (eds) *Handbook of criminal Investigation*. Cullompton, Devon: Willan Publishing, pp 15–41.

Morrish, R. (1940) *The police and crime-detection today*. Oxford: Oxford University Press.

MPS (2017) 'Detective Constable direct entry scheme'. Available at: www.met.police.uk/careers-at-the-met/police-officer-roles/detective-constable/overview/

National Audit Office (2008) *The Independent Police Complaints Commission.* HC1035 session. The Stationery Office, 2007–2008.

Newburn, T, and Reiner, R. (2004) 'From PC Dixon to Dixon PLC: policing and police powers since 1954'. *Criminal Law Review,* August: 601–18.

Neyroud, P. (2008) 'Past, present and future performance: lessons and prospects for the measurement of police performance'. *Policing,* 2(3): 340–48.

Neyroud, P. and Disley, E. (2007) 'The management, supervision and oversight of criminal investigations', in Newburn, T., Williamson, T. and Wright, A. (eds) *Handbook of criminal investigation.* Cullompton, Devon: Willan Publishing, pp 549–71.

Niblett, J. (1997) *Disclosure in criminal proceedings.* London: Blackstone.

Nickerson, R.S. (1998) 'Confirmation bias: a ubiquitous phenomenon in many guises'. *Review of General Psychology,* 2(2): 175–220.

NPCC (2016) *Chief Constables Council Minutes,* pp 1–21. Available at: www.npcc.police.uk/documents/CCCouncilMinutes/2016/Chief%20Constables%20Council%20Minutes%20V5%20External.pdf

NPIA (2007) The Professionalising Investigation Programme. [Online] http://www.npia.police.uk/en/10093.htm

NPIA (2012) Personal safety manual: conflict management. Wyboston, Bedfordshire. Unpublished

O'Hara, C. (1970) *Fundamentals of criminal investigation.* Springfield, IL: Charles Thomas.

O'Neill, M. (2011) *What makes a successful volume crime investigator?* Unpublished PhD thesis, University of Portsmouth.

O'Neill, M. (in press) 'The art and science of investigation', in Griffiths, A, and Milne, B (eds) *Investigation: Psychology into practice.* Abingdon: Routledge.

O'Neill, M. and Milne, B. (2014) 'Success within criminal investigations: is communication still a key component?', in Bull, R. (ed.) *Investigative interviewing.* New York: Springer, pp 123–46.

ONS (2016) *Domestic abuse in England and Wales: Year ending March 2016.* Office for National Statistics. Available at: www.ons.gov.uk/peoplepopulationandcommunity/crimeandjustice/bulletins/domesticabuseinenglandandwales/yearendingmarch2016

Ormerod, D. and Laird, K. (2015) *Smith and Hogan's Criminal Law,* 14th edn. Oxford: Oxford University Press.

Osterburg, J.W. and Ward, R.H. (2000) *Criminal investigation: A method of reconstructing the past*, 3rd edn. Cincinnati, OH: Anderson Publishing Co.

Oxburgh, G. (2015) *Communication in investigative and legal contexts: Integrated approaches from forensic psychology, linguistics and law enforcement.* Chichester: John Wiley & Sons.

Patrick, R. (2011a) '"Reading tea leaves": an assessment of the reliability of police recorded crime statistics'. *The Police Journal*, 84(1): 47–68.

Patrick, R. (2011b) '"A nod and a wink": do "gaming practices" provide an insight into the organizational nature of police corruption?' *The Police Journal*, 84(3): 199–221.

Philips, Sir C. (1982) Royal Commission on Criminal Procedure (Cmnd 8092). London: HMSO.

Phillips, D. (2002) 'The route to professionalism', *Policing Today*, 9: 5–6.

Porter, L.E. and Prenzler, T. (2012) 'Police oversight in the United Kingdom: the balance of independence and collaboration'. *International Journal of Law, Crime and Justice*, 40(3): 152–71.

Poyser, S. and Milne, R. (2015) 'No grounds for complacency and plenty for continued vigilance: miscarriages of justice as drivers for research on reforming the investigative interviewing process'. *The Police Journal*, 88(4): 265–80.

Punch, M. (1983) 'Officers and men: Occupational culture, inter-rank antagonism, and the investigation of corruption', in M. Punch (ed.) *Control in the police organization*, Cambridge, MA: MIT Press, pp 227–50.

Ramsland, K. (2014) *Beating the devil's game: A history of forensic science and criminal investigation.* London: Penguin.

Rassin, E. (2010) Blindness to alternative scenarios in evidence evaluation. *Journal of Investigative Psychology and Offender Profiling*, 7(2): 153–63.

Refuge (2016) *About domestic violence.* Available at: www.refuge.org.uk/about-domestic-violence/#q34

Reiner, R. (1998) 'Problems of assessing individual police performance', in Brodeur, J.P. (ed.) *How to recognise good policing.* London: Sage, pp 55–72.

Reiner, R. (2008) 'Policing and the media' in Newburn, T. (ed.) *Handbook of policing.* Cullompton: Willan Publishing.

Repetto, T.A. (1978) 'The detective task: the state of the art, science craft?' *Police Studies: The International Review of Police Development*, 1(3): 5–10.

Richards, L., Letchford, S. and Stratton, S. (2008) *Policing domestic violence.* Oxford: Oxford University Press.

Roberts, P. (2007) 'Law and criminal investigation', in Newburn, T., Williamson, T. and Wright, A. (eds) *Handbook of criminal investigation.* Cullompton, Devon: Willan Publishing, pp 92–145.

Robinson, A. and Tilley, N. (2009) 'Factors influencing police performance in the investigation of volume crimes in England and Wales'. *Police Practice and Research: An International Journal,* 10(3): 209–23.

Robinson, A.L., Pinchevsky, G.M. and Guthrie, J.A. (2016) 'A small constellation: risk factors informing police perceptions of domestic abuse'. *Policing and Society,* online article, available at: http://dx.doi.org/10.1080/10439463.2016.1151881

Rogers, C. and Gravelle, J. (2012) 'Policing after Winsor: Outsourcing and the Future of Policing'. *The Police Journal,* 85(4): 273–84.

Rook, P. and Ward, R. (2014) *Sexual offences: Law and practice.* London: Sweet and Maxwell.

Rossomo, K.D. (2008) *Criminal investigative failures.* Boca Raton, FL: CRC Press.

Runciman, L. (1993) Report of the Royal Commission on Criminal Justice. Cm. 2262. HMSO.

Salet, R. and Terpstra, J. (2014) 'Critical review in criminal investigation: evaluation of a measure to prevent tunnel vision'. *Policing,* 8(1): 43–50.

Sanders, A. (1977) *Detective work: A study of criminal investigations.* New York: The Free Press.

Sanders, A, and Young, R. (2006) *Criminal justice.* (3rd edn). Oxford: Oxford University Press.

Savage, S.P. (2013) 'Seeking "civilianness" police complaints and the civilian control model of oversight'. *British Journal of Criminology,* 53(5): 886–904.

Savage, S.P. and Milne, B. (2007) 'Miscarriages of justice', in Newburn, T., Williamson, T. and Wright, A. (eds) *Handbook of criminal Investigation.* Cullompton, Devon: Willan Publishing, pp 610–27.

Select Committee on Home Affairs (2005) Fourth Report 2004–2005 session. Annex: The National Centre for Policing Excellence. Available at: www.publications.parliament.uk/pa/cm200405/cmselect/cmhaff/370/37002.htm

Shane, J.M. (2010) 'Organizational stressors and police performance'. *Journal of Criminal Justice,* 38(4): 807–18.

Sharpe, S. (1999) 'Disclosure, immunity and fair trials'. *Journal of Criminal Law,* 63(1): 67–82.

Shepherd, E. and Griffiths, A. (2013) *Investigative interviewing: The Conversation Management Approach.* Oxford: Oxford University Press.

Sheptycki, J. (2004) 'Organizational pathologies in police intelligence systems: some contributions to the lexicon of intelligence-led policing'. *European Journal of Criminology*, 1(3): 307–32.

Sherman, L.W. (2015) 'A tipping point for "totally evidenced policing": ten ideas for building an evidence-based police agency'. *International Criminal Justice Review*, 25(1): 11–29.

Shpayer-Makov, H. (2011) *The ascent of the detective: Police sleuths in Victorian and Edwardian England*. Oxford: Oxford University Press.

Skolnick, J. (1966) *Justice without trial*. New York, NY: Wiley & Sons.

Smith, G. (2009) 'Citizen oversight of independent police services: bifurcated accountability, regulation creep, and lesson learning'. *Regulation and Governance*, 3(4): 421–41.

Smith, N., and Flanagan, C. (2000) *The effective detective: Identifying the skills of an effective SIO*. Police Research Series, No. 122. London: Home Office.

Smith, D.J. and Gray, J. (1983) *The Police in Action: Police and People in London*, vol 4. London: Policy Studies Institute.

Snook, B. and Cullen, R.M. (2008) 'Bounded rationality and criminal investigations: Has tunnel vision been wrongfully convicted?', in Rossomo, D.K. (ed.) *Criminal investigative failures*. Boca Raton, FL: CRC Press, pp 71–98.

Soderman, H. and O'Connell, J.J. (1935) *Modern criminal investigation*. London: Bell.

Soukara, S., Bull, R. and Vrij, A. (2002) 'Police detectives' aims regarding their interviews with suspects: any change at the turn of the millennium?' *International Journal of Police Science & Management*, 4(2): 101–14.

Stanley, N. and Humphreys, C. (2014) Multi-agency risk assessment and management for children and families experiencing domestic violence. *Children and youth services review*, 47: 78–85.

Steer, D. (1980) *Uncovering crime: The Police Role*. The Royal Commission on Criminal Procedure Study number 7 (Cmnd 8092). London: HMSO.

Stelfox, P. (2007) 'Professionalising criminal investigation', in Newburn, T., Williamson, T. and Wright, A. (eds) *Handbook of criminal investigation*. Cullompton: Willan Publishing, pp 628–52.

Stelfox, P. (2009) *Criminal investigation: An introduction to principles and practice*. Cullompton: Willan Publishing.

Stelfox, P. and Pease, K. (2005) 'Cognition and detection: reluctant bedfellows?', in Smith, M. and Tilley, N. (eds) *Crime science: New approaches to preventing and detecting crime*. Cullompton: Willan Publishing.

Stephenson, G.M. and Moston, S. (1994) 'Police interrogation'. *Psychology, Crime and Law*, 1: 151–7.

Stern, Baroness V. (2010) *The Stern Review: An independent review into how rape complaints are handled by public authorities in England and Wales*. London: Government Equalities Office and Home Office.

Stevenson, K. (2004) *Blackstone's guide to the Sexual Offences Act 2003*. Oxford: Oxford University Press.

Taylor, C. (2001) 'Advance disclosure: reflections on the Criminal Procedure and Investigations Act 1996'. *The Howard Journal*, 40(2): 114–25.

Taylor, C. W. (2006) *Criminal investigation and pre-trial disclosure in the United Kingdom. How detectives put together a case*. Lampeter: Edwin Mellen Press Ltd.

Temkin, J. and Krahé, B. (2008) *Sexual assault and the justice gap: A question of attitude*. London: Bloomsbury Publishing.

Tilley, N., Robinson, A. and Burrows, J. (2007) 'The investigation of high volume crime', in Newburn, T., Williamson, T. and Wright, A. (eds) *Handbook of criminal investigation*. Cullompton: Willan Publishing, pp 226–54.

Tong, S. (2005) *Training the effective detective: a case-study examining the role of training in learning to be a detective*. Ph.D. thesis, University of Cambridge.

Tong, S. and Bowling, B. (2006) 'Art, craft and science of detective work'. *The Police Journal*, 79(4): 323–9.

Tong, S. and Wood, D. (2011) 'Graduate police officers: releasing the potential for pre-employment university programmes for aspiring officers'. *The Police Journal*, 84(1): 69-74.

Tong, S., Horvath, M. and Bryant, R. (2009) *Understanding criminal investigation*. Oxford: Wiley-Blackwell.

Turnbull, P.J. and Wass, V. (2015) 'Normalizing extreme work in the police service? Austerity and the inspecting ranks'. *Organization*, 22(4): 512–29.

Tversky, A. and Kahneman, D. (1974) 'Judgment under uncertainty: heuristics and biases'. *Science, New Series*, 185(4157): 1124–31.

Valentine, J. (1935) 'Introduction', in Soderman, H. and O'Connell, J.J. (1935) *Modern criminal investigation*. London: Bell.

van Koppen, P.J. (2008) 'Blundering justice: the Schiedam Park murder', in Kocsis, R.N. (ed.) *Serial murder and the psychology of violent crimes*. Totowa, NJ: Humana, pp 207–28.

Waddington, P.A.J. (2015) 'Learning lessons'. *Policing*, 9(2): 117–18.

Wambaugh, J. (1990) *The blooding*. London: Bantam books.

West, A. (2001) 'A proposal for an investigative science course: any takers?' *Police Research and Management*, 5: 13–22.

Westera, N.J., Kebbell, M., Milne, R., Green, T. (2014) 'Towards a more effective detective. Policing and society.' *An International Journal of Research and Policy*, 26(1): 1–17.

Weston, P.B. and Lushbaugh, C.A. (2012) *Criminal investigation: Basic perspectives*. Upper Saddle River, NJ: Prentice Hall.

White, A. (2014) 'Post-crisis policing and public–private partnerships: the case of Lincolnshire police and G4S'. *British Journal of Criminology*, 54(6): 1002–22.

Williams, S.W.J. (ed.) (1929) *Moriarty's police law*. Oxford: Butterworths.

Williams, V.L. and Sumrall, R.O. (1982) 'Productivity measures in the criminal investigation function'. *Journal of Criminal Justice*, 10(2): 111–22.

Williamson, T. (2007) 'Psychology and criminal investigation', in Newburn, T., Williamson, T. and Wright, A. (eds) *Handbook of criminal investigation*. Cullompton, Devon: Willan Publishing, pp 68–92.

Williamson, T., Newburn, T. and Wright, A. (2007) 'The future of criminal investigation', in Newburn, T., Williamson, T. and Wright, A. (eds) *Handbook of criminal investigation*. Cullompton: Willan Publishing, pp 652–57.

Willis, J.J. (2013) *Improving police: What's craft got to do with it? Ideas in American policing*. The Police Foundation. Available at: www.policefoundation.org/docs/library.html

Willis, J.J. and Mastrofski, S.D. (2016) 'Improving policing by integrating craft and science: what can patrol officers teach us about good police work?' *Policing and Society*. Abingdon: Routledge. DOI: 10.1080/10439463.2015.1135921.

Wilson, J.Q. (1978) *The investigators: Managing FBI and narcotics agents*. New York, NY: Basic Books (AZ).

Wood, D.A., Cockroft, T., Tong, S. and Bryant, R. (2017) 'The importance of context and cognitive agency in developing police knowledge: going beyond the police science discourse'. *The Police Journal*. Available at: http://journals.sagepub.com/doi/abs/10.1177/0032258X17696101

Wright, M. (2013) 'Homicide detectives' intuition'. *Journal of Investigative Psychology and Offender Profiling*, 10(2): 182–99.

Young, M. (1991) *An inside job: Policing and police culture in Britain*. Oxford: Clarendon.

Zander, M. (1979) 'Investigation of crime: a study of cases tried at the Old Bailey'. *Criminal Law Review* (APR), pp 203–19.

Acts and legal cases

Acts

CPIA (1996a) Criminal Procedure and Investigations Act. London: HMSO.

CPIA (1996b) Criminal Procedure and Investigations Act Codes of Practice. London: HMSO.

Human Rights Act 1998. London: HMSO.

Investigatory Powers Act 2016. London: HMSO.

Police and Criminal Evidence Act (PACE) 1984. London: HMSO.

Police Reform Act 2002. London: HMSO.

Regulation of Investigatory Powers Act 2000. London: HMSO.

Sexual Offences Act 2003. London: HMSO.

Legal cases

Bolam v Friern Hospital Management Committee [1957] 2 All ER 118

Osman v United Kingdom [1998] EHRR 101

R v Bree [2007] EWCA Crim 804.

R v Hanson: R v Gilmore: R v Pickstone [2005] EWCA Crim 824.

R v Kiszko (1992) The Times, 18 February 1992.

R v Metropolitan Police Commissioner, ex parte Blackburn [1968] 1 All ER 763

R v Stagg, unreported, 19th September 1994, Central Criminal Court.

R v Taylor (Michelle) 1994 98 Cr.App.R. 361 CA.

R v Turnbull (1977) QB 224.

R v Ward (1993) 96 Cr.App.R. 1 CA.

Appendix

Figure A.1: Dimensions of criminal investigation (revised)

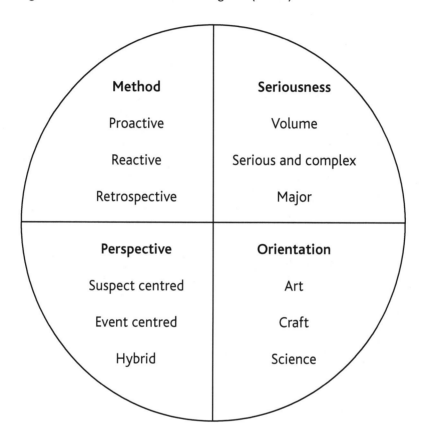

Index

College of Policing (CoP) 9, 17, 53, 55, 56, 71, 75, 76, 79, 80, 81, 83, 91, 93, 98
/HMIC/IPCC concordant 126–7
code of ethics 43, 83
continuing professional development (CPD) 56, 57
creation 21, 43
lack of recognition and respect for 57, 83, 146
record-keeping 81, 135
shift back to dominance of craft in investigations 61, 145, 146
training and higher education 57–8, 60, 100
'compliance drift' 89
Confait, Maxwell 47, 68
confirmatory bias (CB) 67–70
Conflict Management Model (CMM) 78, 79–80
comparing NDM and 79–80, 80
continuing professional development (CPD) 56–7, 98, 102
CoP
see College of Policing (CoP)
Core Investigative Doctrine (CD) 17, 18, 65, 74–7, 148
criticism of 35
use of intuition and creativity 29–30
CPIA (Criminal Procedure and Investigations Act 1996) 4, 12, 13, 81, 92
Codes of Practice 13–15, 17, 98–9
craft dimension 31–2, 42, 44, 61, 145, 146
creativity within investigations 28–9
Criminal Investigation Department (CID) 40, 45, 47, 49, 59, 137, 149
Criminal Justice Act 2003 99–100
Criminal Procedure and Investigations Act 1996 (CPIA) 4, 12, 13, 81, 92
Codes of Practice 13–15, 17, 98–9
Cullen, Katie 141
culture
detective 58
police 39, 58, 134

D

DA
see domestic abuse (DA)
Dean, G. 4, 28, 29
decision-making 65–84, 147–8
ACCESS model 79
accountability 71, 81–2
confirmatory bias (CB) 67–70
Conflict Management Model (CMM) 78, 79–80
convinced of suspect guilt 69

Core Investigative Doctrine (CD) 65, 74–7
creativity and 28–9
and decisions not to invoke criminal process 71
explanation-based decision-making (EBDM) 66–7
heuristics and 67
jury 66–7
Murder Investigation Manual (MIM) 72–4
National Decision Model (NDM) 78–83
naturalistic 65–6
PLAN model 78
PLANE 78
policy files 82, 135
practice 72–7
and professional discretion 81
proportional justice 77
recording 71, 81–2
research 65–72
SARA model 78
scientific method applied to investigative 35–7
stages of process 75, 75
study of detectives own processes 77
tipping points in investigations 68–9
traps 67–8
tunnel vision 70
defining criminal investigation 10–13
statutory definition 13–15
Desborough Committee 45, 46, 145–6
detection rates 106–7
alternatives to measuring success by 107, 108, 112, 117
investigative method and 24
problems with measuring success by 41, 113–14
variations in 109–10
dimensions of criminal investigation 8–9, 10, 36
revised 36, 175
direct entry detective recruitment 41, 55, 59, 149
disclosure malpractice 13
discretion, professional 81, 90–1
championing of greater 78, 80, 81, 83, 142, 149
problems with increasing 148–9
DNA 32, 33, 70
domestic abuse (DA)
calls 92, 140
lack of resources and failings in managing 137
need for better training in managing 141, 142
reclassification of high-risk victims 142
recorded crimes 140